# YOU GROW GIRL

## THE GROUNDBREAKING GUIDE TO GARDENING

by Gayla Trail

illustrations by Leela Corman

A FIRESIDE BOOK PUBLISHED BY SIMON & SCHUSTER
NEW YORK   LONDON   TORONTO   SYDNEY

Fireside
Rockefeller Center
1230 Avenue of the Americas
New York, NY 10020

For information about special discounts for bulk purchases,
please contact Simon & Schuster Special Sales:
1-800-456-6798 or business@simonandschuster.com

Designed by Gayla Trail, Fluffco Design, Toronto, Canada
Illustrations copyright © 2005 by Leela Corman
A Sockit Projects Book

Manufactured in the United States of America
9    10
Library of Congress Cataloging-in-Publication Data
Trail,Gayla.
You grow girl : the groundbreaking guide to gardening / Gayla Trail;
illustrations by Leela Corman.
p. cm.
Includes index.
1. Gardening. I. Corman, Leela. II. Title.
SB453.T7199   2005
635–dc22    2004061972
ISBN-13: 978-0-7432-7014-4
ISBN-10:     0-7432-7014-2

To Scylla Trail and the balcony-grown potatoes that started it all.
And to Davin, my partner and support in all things, including gardening.

# CONTENTS

Legend

Each project is marked to show the difficulty level

easy peasy

no sweat

a good time

roll up your sleeves

get down and dirty

# INTRODUCTION

## IN THE BEGINNING

I first caught the gardening bug at the age of five when I grew my first plant from seed, a tiny parsley in a foam cup. I vividly recall excitedly waking up each morning to check on the progress of that little plant. Had it grown overnight? Did it need water? Was it ready to go outside? When I finally made a home for it in our backyard veggie plot, the pride swelled in me like a pint-sized Bionic Woman. This is what brings most people to gardening or at the very least keeps us coming back for more: curiosity, excitement, and a connection to both ourselves and the big "out there."

I tried my hand at and successfully "grew stuff" a few times over the years but didn't really catch that bug again until the late 1990s, when I began experimenting with the odd plant and some seeds collected from kitchen scraps. Before I knew it my urban deck was littered with pots of this, that, and the next. It was then that I discovered I had a Godzilla-sized hobby on my hands and it was time to pick up a book or two. Boy was I in for a shock. I discovered that there were few publications in any media that appealed to my perspective as a young, frugal urban gardener with no permanent space and only a sweltering hot deck to my name. The gardening world focused on a very specific demographic—older suburban ladies—and I wasn't a part of it. Gardening books took it for granted that I had a sprawling backyard and an eager bank account and wasn't it all so deathly boring! Where was the fun, the childlike wonderment, the cheeseball sense of pride and accomplishment? Everything was so hyperperfect, organized, and restrained. My plans for world domination were suddenly looking awfully meager. I quickly went online to find like-minded individuals and found that even in the world of geeks and freaks there was no space for renegade gardeners to commune. And so in early 2000 **YouGrowGirl.com** was born.

I have always resisted referring to **You Grow Girl** as strictly a gardening site, because it seems to offer so much more. Whatever it is, whether it's a lifestyle choice, a green revolution, or a way to make some pretty, this new style of gardening is about exploration, excitement, and a punk rock approach to growing plants that takes the good stuff from tradition and tosses the rest into the composter.

# GETTING GARDENING FEVER

For decades gardening has been depicted as a crazy hippy notion, a hobby for the rich, or an old-lady pastime. Surely no one under the age of forty would even consider growing a garden, especially if a backyard is nowhere in sight. Gardening was something our grandparents had to do to feed themselves through the Depression. Later our parents took it up under the term "yard work" as a status-seeking tool for keeping up with the Joneses or as a source of sustenance and revenue on pseudo-cultish hippy communes. Those of us who grew up in the suburbs have cultivated a negative experience of gardening, the result of Saturday afternoons spent mowing endless lawns and clipping topiary hedges.

But these days just as knitting, sewing, needlepoint, and so many other femalecentric traditions are coming back into vogue, the younger, hipper set is starting to see the value in taking up the trowel. This time around we have the benefit of choice rather than being forced by necessity or stupid social expectations. Especially in urban centers where greenery is sparse and most people spend their days chained to a computer screen, people are discovering that not only can nature co-exist with city life, but it actually enhances it. A garden, whether it be a half-acre vegetable plot or a little potted flower, can relieve the tension and stress of modern gotta-have-it-yesterday living. Simply looking at a plant is known to lower the heart rate almost instantaneously. Gardening is peaceful, relaxing, and good exercise for both the brain and the bod. It builds patience and cultivates a sense of pride and do-it-yourself self-reliance. Gardening has been called both "the new yoga" and "the new rock 'n' roll." I think it's both!

My approach to gardening and this book begins with this piece of advice: follow your heart. Begin with what comes easy to you—whether you're a crafty chick, a DIY freak, or an obsessive planner. Go from there and work your way to the harder, less intuitive stuff. Gardening as a whole can appear quite intimidating from the outside. It seems like there is an endless amount of knowledge to acquire and challenges to face. But honestly, when it comes down to it, the knowledge you need to start growing one or three plants is actually quite minimal. Gardening is really just an ongoing experiment with a method that is more trial and error than set in stone. If your strong suit is on the technical end of things, then you're probably into growing seeds, learning Latin names for your plants, and messing about in the soil. Testing for pH and analyzing your soil contents is definitely the place to start. Once you've built up your confidence by focusing on the things you love, working your way toward the artistic end of the spectrum will be a breeze. Artsy types on the other hand will have little trouble inventing theme gardens, putting colors together, or making cool pots and accessories. You should start out by sewing a groovy garden apron, making some stepping-stones, or designing your garden plan.

This book can be read linearly as a start-to-finish guide, or randomly. Flip through the pages and jump right in where something exciting catches your eye. Where you start and where you go from there are up to you. There are no rules.

This book provides all the basics that you need to begin and maintain a healthy organic garden. It also includes a wealth of creative crafts and projects. Reading the book straight through from start to finish will guide you through the process, from starting a new garden to putting your garden to bed at the end of the season. I've broken it down into five chapters.

## Plan

This chapter begins with learning about your current space (or finding one), teaching you how to make an initial assessment, and showing you how to expand on what you've got to make the most of it. I cover the ins and outs of making a plan or scrapping the formality entirely and give you some out-there ideas for finding inspiration and making a cool garden that reflects your personal style and taste. The chapter includes projects that guide you through gardening in tough spaces, how to choose the right plants for your garden, where to get good plants cheap, and how to make the most of what you've got. For the gardener without a garden, tips are provided for creating a super-fabulous container garden from bland ready-made pots and terrific trash.

## Plant

The second chapter is all about getting those gorgeous plants into the soil—whether that's in a sprawling backyard, on a rickety fire escape, or on a narrow window ledge. We begin first with the crazy world of soil: the different types, how to recognize and test it, and how to make it the best dirt ever. The chapter also includes a handy field guide to can't-live-without-them garden tools and a thorough seed-starting primer with frugal tips for getting supplies and keeping the seedlings happy. Projects include how to set up a killer window-box garden, sew a groovy garden apron, grow seeds in Jell-O, and build a professional-style planter box.

## Grow

The third chapter covers the nuts and bolts of keeping the plants under your watch healthy and happy. The how, when, and what of daunting tasks like fertilizing, pruning, staking, and composting are clarified. You'll learn how to do things in small spaces you never thought possible, like making compost and growing tasty food crops, ornamental plants, and herbal teas. Effective pest prevention techniques, safe, homemade pesticides, and disease remedies are available for when trouble finds your happy garden. Grow a carnivorous plant bog on your deck, protect your strawberries with a homemade cloche, or grow a garden for your favorite feline friend.

## Bounty

No doubt the best part of gardening is hauling in the goods. The fourth chapter leads you through the harvesting process and offers suggestions for putting it all to use. Follow instructions on how to prepare and preserve your crops and propagate new plants free. Lose that go-nowhere dependence on the seed man and find out how to save seeds from your own plants and the methods for storing them properly that will keep you and your friends in seeds for a long time to come. If you're excited about what to do with your bounty, this chapter gives you projects for turning herbs into lush, homemade bath and beauty products and tips for getting bigger crops.

## Chill

Here's where it gets tricky. The gardening season may be coming to an abrupt end or simply going on hold for a month or two. What do you do? The last chapter is all about coping with the seasons and preparing your garden for the big chill. Find out how to clean up the garden, store your precious pots, and even grow winter crops. And when that's all done there are projects to carry you through the down months and get you excited about starting all over next season—when your garden will be even bigger and badder!

Whether you're a sprouting or a seasoned gardener, I hope this book inspires you to experiment, explore, and try something new. Remember, there is no perfection or failure when it comes to gardening—only learning and process. Go out there fearlessly and get some dirt under your nails!

# PLAN

Your garden can be absolutely anything you can dream up, from a field of native wildflowers in the front yard to a Johnny-jump-up planted in an old boot. I've seen everything from a hillside of gorgeous desert succulents to a slightly over-the-top patriotic planting of red, white, and blue (U.S.A) flowers.

Some planning and forethought are important if you want to transform a forlorn patch of dirt into your own private Eden. But many beginners go overboard sweating the planning, intimidating themselves right out of the fun. During the off-season I construct elaborate fantasy gardens and make obsessive to-do lists that I quickly toss out the window come spring in favor of impulse plant purchases and dirty fingernails. I recommend starting with the projects that bring you the most joy and working your way up to trickier challenges. Enjoy some success with a potted geranium before tackling the whole backyard. If decorating and crafting is your thing, you can start by making some stepping-stones or painting some pots, then work your way up to a monumental garden design.

Remember that a garden is always a work in progress with no definable end. It can be just a couple of herbs on a windowsill and still count! Accepting that you can make changes as you learn will take some of the pressure off and make room for experimentation and spontaneity. If you don't like the eight-foot swath of clover leading up to a granite dolphin statue that seemed so cool last year, you can always pull it up and start again. Save the formal garden for later and focus on expressing your creativity and personal style now. And have a blast doing it!

This chapter leads you through some of the potentially intimidating aspects of planning and prepping, from making wise choices at the garden center and decoding the secret language of plant tags to getting your favorite plants cheap, and it will get you rolling on creating your own dream garden.

# SPACES AND PLACES

Popular gardening books and television shows claim to inspire solutions to the small-space dilemma. But their idea of small is my idea of a Versailles! To most city and apartment dwellers, outdoor space equals a small deck, a postage-stamp yard, a fire escape, or even worse—merely a window that opens. Don't despair! What you don't have in space, you can make up for with creativity and imagination, and by breaking a few rules.

Think outside the norm! Who says front yards must be lawn or that veggies can be grown only in the backyard? If all you have is a front yard, why not dig it up and put in a vegetable or flower garden? Bushes or fences can do double duty to create privacy from the street for the sit-down garden of your dreams, even if your yard is on a busy intersection.

If you're calling a fire escape "the yard," make use of vertical space and hang boxes off the rails. Nothing but a window? That ledge is begging for a window-box herb garden.

A garden can happen anywhere. All it takes is a plant and a dream.

## WHATCHA GOT

Most gardening magazines are chockablock full of gorgeous photos of lush, vibrant, immaculately kept gardens. It's gorgeous and you want it.

What they don't tell you is that some gardens are damn hard work to build and even harder to maintain. They also fail to mention that they have teams of trained gardeners keeping those places spotless—at least for the photo shoot! Even harder than attaining the Perfect Garden is trying to create a garden that does not suit your environment. Face it, an English cottage garden full of water-loving perennials is going to be difficult to achieve in Las Vegas. You'd have to change the soil completely, create shade, water, water, water, and sprinkle magic dust on the yard. However, a garden filled with gorgeous desert plants is a snap in Nevada because the perfect conditions are already in place.

Identifying the advantages of your space and working with them is smart (and fun!) gardening. Look at what you've got, take stock of the problems around you, and see how they can be put to good use or worked around. Learn to identify conditions within your own space that will affect how your plants grow. Knowing what you've got will save a lot of heartache and may generate some happy surprise opportunities. The following are assets and problem points to ponder before you dip your shovel in the soil.

## Perfect Plants for a Fire Escape

Fire escapes are a particularly harsh environment—windy, intensely hot, and dry. The metal soaks up heat and reflects it twofold onto plants. But if it's all you've got, go for it! I've seen fire-escape gardens with climbing vines and hanging plants that could put a suburbanite to shame.

The key is to water, water, water. In the heat of summer you'll have to water your plants daily (or more). Choose varieties that can take the heat and then some. Try:

* Coreopsis
* Dahlberg daisy (*Dyssodia tenuiloba*)
* Hens and chicks
* Lavender
* Marigold
* Morning glory
* Passionflower (*Passiflora* species)
* Portulaca
* Rosemary
* Salvia
* Scented geranium 'Attar of Roses' (*Pelargonium capitatum*)
* Sedum
* Tomatillo
* Tomato
* Zinnia

## Light

The direction your garden faces plays a role in how much light it receives and when. The ideal and most versatile direction is south facing, because the garden will receive sun throughout the day. You can always create shade, but you can't magically conjure up more sunshine.

Take a look around and see if you can make some easy changes to achieve the best light in your space. Sometimes all it takes is pruning a few branches. And of course many trees don't get their leaves until late spring, allowing a bit of time to go nuts with early-spring-flowering plants and bulbs. If even on the best of days you don't get a lot of light, don't despair, lots of gorgeous plants thrive in shady conditions. A woodland garden is exciting in its own right.

## Zones

At the back of each and every gardening book (including this one!) is a rainbow-striped map that divides North America according to climate conditions. Hardiness zones tell you which plants can survive year-round and unprotected in your general area. Knowing your zone supposedly makes gardening a breeze. What can and can't be grown in your garden is predetermined by an assigned zone number. All you have to do is pick plants that correspond to your zone number, and you've got a garden. But it doesn't really work that way. My own zone is completely inconsistent from map to map and chart to chart. Some books say as low as 4, while others go as high as 6!

The zone chart is a guideline that should not be taken too literally. Since microclimates (see below) can quite radically alter conditions even within the same small garden, it is impossible to categorize an entire region. Knowing your zone is a good starting point. If the plant tag says zone 10 and you're in zone 3, you can pretty safely forget it. However, a zone 6 garden can easily be adapted to accommodate plants listed a zone above or below. As you work within your garden you will become more familiar with the subtle nuances and rely less and less on sweeping generalizations.

Of course, indoor spaces are not under zone chart jurisdiction. A warm winter retreat indoors can extend the growing season of warm-climate plants regardless of the conditions outside.

## Microclimates

The city is a unique, artificial environment with many variables that can affect gardening conditions within small areas. An abundance of tarmac, brick, and concrete absorbs heat all day long and releases it at night. Glass and metal surfaces

## Zoning Out

Don't let zone charts cramp your style. You can bust out, go wild, and grow plants listed well south of your zone in your garden. Just dig them up and put them in a container for indoor living during the winter. I grow tender pineapple sage and lemon verbena (normally zones 8–10) in a pot on my zone 5 deck. They're happy and healthy in a sunny window in my heated apartment all winter long and hit the deck when spring comes.

Growing cold-zone plants in tropical locations is another deal entirely. In this case, the solution means giving your plant a vacation in the fridge where it can get the cold spell it needs before a sunny summer outdoors.

reflect light and heat, bouncing it from place to place. Vehicles, industry, buildings, and houses all generate heat, working together to raise the temperature by a few degrees. In contrast, buildings, walls, and other large, flat surfaces sometimes create shaded, cooler conditions. Buildings also affect how and where rain falls and can block wind or push it between buildings creating a wind tunnel effect.

You don't have to live in a city to experience microclimates. A paved patio, tall fence, tree, or even a koi pond can alter the conditions within a garden, making it warmer, cooler, wetter, or drier than the spaces nearby.

Microclimates can be a pain in the neck or a fantastic advantage, depending on your perspective. Sometimes it's a matter of a little experimentation to discover what works and what doesn't within a space. Some plants will appreciate the added warmth of a brick wall, while others will fade and wilt at the extra heat. This is where guides such as the USDA Plant Hardiness Zone Map fall apart. While an entire city or region may be shown as one zone, it is possible to cheat the system intentionally or by accident within the tiniest space. I say, if conditions aren't right for a plant in one spot, turn a corner!

Instead of following generalizations, look around at what your neighbors are growing and where. Better yet, ask them about their challenges and successes. Gardeners are often happy to share their tips and experiences with others. We're all garden geeks at heart!

## Pollution

Pollution sucks, but its only real impact on your garden is whether or not you decide to grow edibles. Is your garden next to a busy street? Exhaust fumes from heavy traffic can choke out tender plants or sprinkle a dusting of unidentified brown filth. Probably not something you want on your eggplant.

If you are planning to grow in the ground, look around at the buildings in your area and, if possible, find out what was on your land before you got there. Cities evolve and change rapidly over the years, leaving their mark in the soil that remains. What was an industrial wasteland yesterday is tomorrow's townhome lofts. Gas stations, factories, old homes, paint shops, and old dump sites are particularly nasty culprits, leaving behind a legacy of lead and other toxins. If in doubt, get your soil tested (see page 22).

## Wind

Wind is an evil torture device for every city gardener. Exposed rooftops can feel like a full-time hurricane, especially in early spring and fall. Cracks between buildings also create prime conditions for a tunnel effect that sweeps high wind and garbage through the gap.

High winds can burn and dry out a plant worse than scorching midday sun. They will also knock over insecure or unbalanced container plants—especially trees and pots of tall beans. In the garden, high winds contribute to soil erosion and scare off beneficial insects.

Don't get bummed. Even wind can be worked around. In exposed areas, plan your garden around wind protection. One way is to create a living shield of large, hardy, and wind-tolerant plants on the outside with sensitive plants protected on the inside. There's strength in numbers—grouping containers together will help prevent them from falling over. Try growing a row of evergreen trees or shrubs to act as a living barrier to high winds. Dwarf varieties of boxwood and azaleas do well in large containers on exposed rooftops. In southern climates, opt for bamboo hedges or eucalyptus.

## Wild Animals

While you can't exactly plan ahead for pests, keep in mind that no matter where you are you will encounter them. Pests come in two different varieties, country and city, each with its own set of challenges and temperaments. Country pests tend to walk on four feet and love to dig in the dirt and eat tender leaves and fresh produce ripe off the vine. Everyone has a tried-and-true method for fending off raccoons, deer, rabbits, and other critters that range from the bizarre (sprinkling human hair and urine across the garden) to the old-fashioned (scarecrows). The good thing is that country pests are generally afraid of humans. Creating barriers and fences around the garden seems to be the most effective, long-lasting method in large open spaces. You may also need to accept a little loss now and again to the one that gets away, so factor a percentage of that into your plans.

City pests are another thing entirely, coming in unexpected shapes and sizes and often walking on two feet. It's hard to believe but your fabulously fantastic garden may not get the respect it deserves from others, including your own neighbors. Some people just don't notice gardens and will throw litter into yours simply because they don't *get* it. Others see the privacy of a shrub or tall plant as a convenient public toilet. I am well acquainted with the human pest but have yet to come up with the perfect solution. Low fences help, but if you are planning a garden in a high-traffic area, expect a few rounds of garbage-picking duty in addition to weeding chores. You can also count on some trampled foliage and ripped stems. Save the super spectacular or expensive flowers for the backyard. Passers-by can't resist helping themselves to dazzling sunflowers and lilies.

Critters of the four-legged variety are equally difficult. City pests completely lack a healthy fear of humans and will get into everything, unwavering even when confronted. No matter how menacingly I stomp and wave my broom, Rocky the Raccoon continues to sit and stare as if to say "Yeah, right." (See page 118 for more solutions.)

## Borrowed Land

Community gardens provide a wonderful utopian opportunity for green thumbs (or wanna-be green thumbs) with no outdoor space of their own to get their garden on.

Since the 1970s when Green Was Good, most cities, towns, and some suburbs have set land aside in parks or on community property where locals can garden. Anyone can sign up for a plot at the community gardens, pay a small fee, and call it their own. It's a great way to meet other gardeners, learn from the ol' pros, and grow fancy plants that don't have a chance in your window box garden.

## Flower Power

Community gardens have a way of transforming derelict spaces as well as energizing community pride and support. In the late 1970s, community groups in New York City's East Village turned garbage-strewn empty lots into blooming urban oases. Skip ahead a decade or so and the once ignored area began to look pretty good to property developers and like easy money for the city. Not ready to go down without a fight, the community rose up in protest, battling for the gardens they had worked hard to build and grow. In the eleventh hour before the land was to be auctioned off to the highest bidder, actress Bette Midler and two environmental groups raised enough money to buy the land and protect the gardens.

Community gardening plots follow a few different models, so find out if your local garden's rules jive with your gardening style before you sign up. The web can help you to find the community garden in your 'hood (see Resources).

If the wait is too long for your local garden, or if the 1970s never happened in your area, consider starting your own community garden. Most cities and towns are chock full of fallow land and unused, wasted spaces desperate to be transformed into gorgeous gardens. Locate land in your area that seems ripe for a green take over, then find some cohorts who are willing to put some effort into making a garden happen. Don't be shy, contact the owner (the owner might be the city or town!) to request permission. It may take some time, but if you keep asking you will eventually find an owner who sees the benefits to the trade. Community gardeners act as stewards of the land, beautifying the area and eventually reducing crime and vandalism. Check out Resources for books and info about community gardens.

## GROWING GUERRILLA

Who says you need a garden to be a gardener? Cities and suburbs are packed with fallow land, empty lots, sidewalk cracks, and "wasted" space ready for planting guerilla-style. Guerrilla gardening is about transforming space to benefit everyone rather than about personal ownership. It's about gardening anywhere and everywhere, using plants to create beauty in forgotten spaces.

Guerrilla gardening doesn't have to be an illicit affair. I have tended a piece of public land along the side of my building for years, and I do it out in the open in the middle of the day. When I moved in, it was a 10-foot by 5-foot chunk of wasted space between the building and the sidewalk that was home to car parts, plastic wrappers, and needles. It is now a lovely little garden and happy home for an assortment of perennials. While the city technically owns the land, I take care of it as if it were my own mini-backyard.

You too can start a green revolution in your neighborhood. Team up with a couple of friends and scope out the abandoned lots, alleys, edges of parking lots, or other neglected spaces nearby. Once you've found your site, all you need are seeds or seedlings, a shovel for digging, some compost, and a bottle of water to help the little guys get a good head start.

When choosing plants, do your homework. Native plants (plants that grow naturally in your climate and environment) are a wise choice because they're easy to grow and can often stand some serious neglect when planted in the right environment. Stay away from invasive plants that will take over and push out any natives currently residing in the space. The idea is to spread some botanical joy, not create a new problem. Veggies and other edibles will work too, but might require a return visit or two for maintenance. Of course, if your guerrilla action is seeding a sidewalk crack, anything that can withstand such a harsh environment is welcome. Try annual seeds such as sunflowers, pansies, cosmos, calendula, and marigolds. Remember, seeds collected from your own garden are free and plentiful, so you and your Green Team can go wild without breaking the bank!

# DEFINING SPACE

Fences and barriers are useful tools that have more than aesthetic value in any garden. In large suburban or country gardens they divide open expanses into manageable sections, keep out pests, and protect plants from harsh natural elements. Big rocks work as points of interest or to hold the soil in where the garden slopes. Tall plants in a row can act as a living wall.

In the city they are all this and more. A bit of privacy away from the chaos is a dreamy notion. Shrubs, evergreens, and even tall annuals (such as sunflowers) provide coverage without caging you in. A trellis bursting with clematis, passionflower, sweet pea flowers, or scarlet runner beans uses nature to block the view of your neighbor's crazy Mount Olympus–themed fountain or the parking lot across the street.

Where traffic is high, barriers let others know to show some respect and back off. It's a bit of reverse psychology, but high fences don't keep vandals out. In many ways they only highlight the fact that there is something of interest lurking behind the fence that they've been locked out of. My own sidewalk garden, located at the corner of a very busy city intersection, suffered a constant barrage of trampling and general destruction during the first four years of its existence. It was regarded as a pile of dirt and treated like a dumping ground for everything from used needles to dead tropical plants (someone thought they might have a second life under my care). Finally I got smart and constructed a low fence. After that everyone in the neighborhood stood up and took notice. I received endless compliments on the garden's beauty and praise for improving the area. Sadly, pretty plants aren't always enough to signify a garden, but a cute, decorative fence is!

## BLAZING TRAILS

Paths are another eye-catching yet functional way to divide space. I use short paths in my small twenty-foot by seven-foot garden to provide access to plants at the back of the garden and to segment the area into pockets of interest. A path invites the eye to wander through the garden and can create a bit of mystery and intrigue in a small space. Natural slate, stone, and decorative tile make lovely paths, but they're also hard on the wallet. Save your money and instead make your paths from broken brick (I found mine piled under the fire escape), bark chips, or broken cement or asphalt. Neighborhoods are full of curbside treasures waiting for a second life in the garden.

Lots of plants can be made into living paths, too. Turn the concept of the front lawn on its head and grow a garden with a few grassy pathways. Or better yet, for stepping-stones substitute "stepping-plants" like creeping thyme (*Thymus serpyllum*), 'Dragon's Blood' clover (*Trifolium repens*), Scotch moss or Irish moss (*Sagina subulata*). If you can't afford a living pathway, grow a few of these plants in the cracks and spaces between steps. Rather than building a tight path, buy a few large stones and space them out.

If crafting is your thing, you can make your own cement stepping-stones using cake pans, margarine containers, or leaves as molds. A bag of cement from the hardware store will make an army of personalized "bricks" for the garden.

# RUSTIC WOVEN TWIG FENCE

Put your summer-camp weaving skills to use to make this charming low-rise edging out of curbside garden waste. It is tall enough to keep off-leash dogs and two-legged intruders from your plants, but low enough to create an unobstructed view of the garden behind it. Not only is it free and natural, it's also much better looking than the tacky plastic edging found in most garden centers.

You can also build a taller free-standing version at the back of the garden as a trellis for clematis and other climbing vines or to screen off areas you'd rather hide from public view.

## You Will Need

∗ 34 thick branches (between 1½ and 2 inches in diameter), approximately 20 inches long to use as posts
∗ Saw or axe
∗ Hammer or rubber mallet
∗ A large bundle of long, flexible branches (approximately 50 branches). Willow is a good choice. Each branch should be approximately 60 to 80 inches long.
∗ Garden shears

**1.** Drive the posts into the ground using a rubber mallet and brute strength. For easier driving, sharpen the post ends ahead of time with a knife (just like whittling) or saw the posts on an angle—but lazy people like me can skip this step entirely. Place the first post at the end of the border. Have a friend hold the post in position while you pound it with a rubber mallet or hammer until it sinks about 5 inches into the soil. The "post holder" might consider wearing gloves as added protection against slippage. This is the most difficult part of the project, as some posts will slip easily into soft soil and others will inevitably come up against rocks.

**2.** Space your posts 10 inches apart. Wider spacing will create a less secure fence. Don't space your posts too close or you'll have difficulty weaving the less flexible branches in later.

step 3

**3.** Starting with the first post, begin weaving the first flexible branch in and out between the posts. When you get to the end of the branch, cut off any extra overhang using garden shears.

**4.** Gently push the woven branch down to the ground and adjust.

**5.** Start at the next empty post with a fresh branch and repeat steps 3 and 4. The trick to starting this next branch is beginning your weave from behind if the previous branch ended in front, and vice versa.

**6.** Once you hit the end of the first row, jump back to the beginning with a new branch. Continue weaving three more rows of branches in the same over-under pattern. Push each branch down against the previous row as you did in step 4 so there are no gaps between rows.

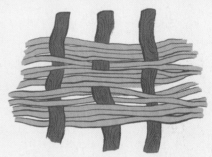

alternate direction of rows

**7.** Once you have woven four rows of branches, switch the direction of your weaves, beginning from the back if your first four rows began from the front and vice versa. As you weave branches in, you will find the fence becoming more secure and taut.

That's it! Remember the charm of this fence is its rustic character and handmade imperfection. Most measurements can be eyeballed. These instructions make a fence 15 inches tall that will surround a 15-foot by 7-foot garden on three sides. Increase or decrease quantities proportionately to make larger or smaller fences.

# HOMEGROWN STONES

Half the fun of having a garden is decorating it to make it your own. Because of this, garden centers are often stocked with just as many useless decorative whatnots as plants and actual useful garden gadgetry. But your conscience (and, let's face it, your wallet) won't let you be suckered in by overpriced knickknacks. Who needs a glow-in-the-dark plastic garden gnome when, with a few cheap materials and absolutely no skill, you can make your own individualized garden decor? These stylish cement stepping-stones make a useful walkway or beautiful decorative garden edging.

## You Will Need

* Real leaves (these are your "molds"); 1 leaf = 1 stone
* Newspaper
* Disposable plastic gloves (protect your hands!)
* Powdered cement mix
* Water
* Large yogurt or margarine container for mixing cement
* Putty knife or old butter knife
* Pieces of cardboard

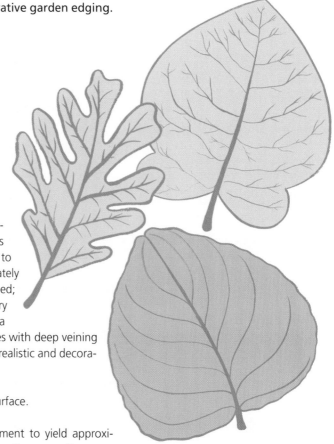

First, locate a free source of fresh, medium-to-large-sized leaves that are at least 4 inches wide and 6 inches long. These leaves will be your "mold." If you're planning to use your stones as a walkway, they should be approximately the size of your foot. Choose leaves that are simply shaped; complex shapes with too many curves and edges are very time-consuming to mold. Maple leaves are an example of a complex leaf shape, while hostas are a simple shape. Leaves with deep veining and interesting textures will result in stones that are highly realistic and decorative, yet easy to produce.

**1.** Lay down a layer of newspaper to protect your work surface.

**2.** Following the directions on the package, mix up cement to yield approximately 2 cups. Aim for a thick consistency that holds rather than runs. Two cups (or half a large yogurt container) is more than enough to make a large leaf stone.

**3.** Lay your first leaf, back side facing up, onto a piece of cardboard. The back side of the leaf is distinguished by more prominent veining. Try to lay your leaf as flat as possible.

**4.** Using a putty or butter knife, scoop cement onto the back of the leaf. Coat the entire leaf, keeping the cement within the leaf shape. Build up the edges to at least ¼ inch thick, mounding more cement toward the center, which should be at least 1½ inches thick. The thicker the cement, the sturdier your final stone will be. Remember, if you're using your stones as a walkway, they will need to withstand the pressure of a person's body weight.

**5.** Using the knife or your gloved hand, smooth around the edges.

**6.** Set your stone aside to dry on the cardboard piece for an hour or two. Repeat from step 2 to make more stones.

**7.** After an hour or two the stone will have partially dried. Turn it over and slowly peel away the leaf. Be sure that the leaf and stone are still a bit wet so it will peel off fairly easily. Fuzzy leaves can be fussy.

**8.** Set your stone aside for a day or two to dry completely and cure. Some cement mixes require longer curing times. Refer to the package for further instructions.

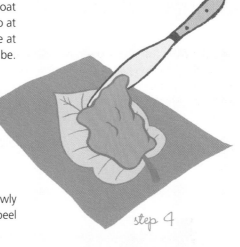

step 4

## More Ideas

＊ You can add powdered dyes to some cement mixes to create naturalistic or crazy-colored leaf stones.

＊ To give stones a mossy, aged look, apply a coat of beer or yogurt to a cured stone. Then rub some dirt from the garden onto the stone and set in a damp, shaded spot for a few months.

step 6

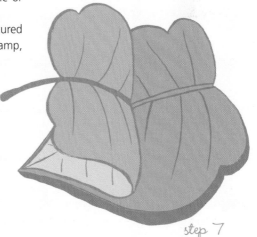

step 7

# WHAT TO DO WITH A CHUNK OF DIRT

Lucky you! You just moved into a great new apartment with an actual yard!

Too bad it's an uninhabitable dump.

Don't worry, just break out the garbage bags and start clearing out the trash. Even if growing edible plants is out of the question, some fresh thinking and elbow grease can turn an uninspiring junk heap into an urban oasis. Try these ideas on for size:

## GARBAGE DUMP CHIC

Make junk work for you. Some junk is cool and adds charm and excitement to a boring garden. The best junk can be kitschy or have a feeling of history.

✳ Scatter bits of broken porcelain as decorative container mulch.
✳ Sink used wine bottles into the ground neck down to create a pathway of colorful circles of glass. It's sturdy and can take the weight of foot traffic.
✳ Line up broken bricks as a border for your garden bed.
✳ Instead of having that broken-down VW bug towed, why not make it into a giant planter?
✳ Construct a wind chime from dug-up rusty nuts and bolts.
✳ Using unidentified rusty metal objects and bits of ceramic thingies, make instant objets d'art, and place them purposefully amidst bushy plants. I once saw a really cool old tree decorated with used utensils, horseshoes, and other rusted metal ephemera.

A good imagination and a small budget can help you to transform junk into useful items. People will pay big bucks at antique fairs for that fancy garbage accumulated in your yard! Old TV antenna towers, rakes, and broken ladders make terrific trellises for vines like clematis and climbing roses. Chairs with broken backs can be gussied up a bit and used to create height for small container plants. Empty containers of all kinds, from oil cans to work boots, make great planters. The key here is to think shabby chic, not *Sanford and Son*.

## DEALING WITH LOUSY SOIL

A successful garden is a healthy one, and the key to a healthy garden is healthy soil. If you want to get the most mileage out of plants, work to build up the nutritional value of your soil over time. (See chapter 2 for detailed descriptions and solutions for soil quality and texture.) But turning over a new leaf can take a lot of time and effort. In the meantime, the following plants tolerate poor soil and will get you started on the road to recovery.

## Testing Soil for Toxicity

For your own safety, have your soil tested before growing edibles. Most toxins are undetectable by sight or smell and many stay in the soil forever. Who knows what went on in your yard fifty years ago that could still be in the soil today? In the United States, contact your county extension office (usually found in the local government section of your phone book). Ask the lab if they test for heavy metals in addition to other toxic chemicals. All you have to do is send a sample of dirt collected from your soil and the lab will do the rest. In a few weeks you should have a list indicating the percentages of various chemicals and toxins in your soil.

## DRY, POOR SOIL

Good soil has a healthy nutritional content, is filled with air pockets, and sucks up moisture well while also draining quickly. But only tough plants that can survive drought conditions and minimal nutritional value can make it in poor, dry soil. Try:

* Beach fleabane (*Erigeron glaucus*)
* Bird's foot trefoil (*Lotus corniculatus*)
* Daylilies (*Hemerocallis*)
* Chinese silvergrass (*Miscanthus floridulus*)
* Cinquefoil (*Potentilla* species)
* Cushion spurge (*Euphorbia polychrome*)
* Globe thistle (*Echinops* species)
* Mexican hyssop (*Agastache mexicana*)
* Red fescue (*Festuca rubra*)
* Sea holly (*Eryngium* species)
* Sweet William (*Dianthus barbatus*)
* Yarrow (*Achillea millefolium*)

## COMPACT SOIL

Compact soil is similar to poor, dry soil only worse. Usually the soil was compressed by excess foot traffic or large vehicles. Compacted soil is a problem in the garden because it means the roots cannot spread easily and are often deprived of proper air circulation. Plants with shallow root systems are best here. Try:

* Clover (*Trifolium repens* 'Dark Dancer' or 'Dragon's Blood')
* Bishop's weed (*Aegopodium podagraria*)
* Low bush honeysuckle (*Diervilla lonicera*)

## WET, POOR SOIL

What's worse than compacted soil? Wet soil that puddles but doesn't drain, that's what. Again, the long-term solution is to build up the humus content of the soil so it holds moisture and nutrition yet does not remain stagnant and sloppy. But achieving that perfect soil can take a long time and a lot of energy. Another good option is to grow a bog. There are lots of incredible and exotic bog plants that will thrive in these conditions. Take your pick from the lists that follow on page 24.

### They Paved Paradise

There's a Talking Heads song that goes "There was a shopping mall. Now it's all covered with flowers…. Once there were parking lots. Now it's a peaceful oasis." I am always reminded of this song as I pass a deserted lot teaming with wildflowers. Nature always finds a way to come back from the worst conditions humans can throw at it. Investigate fallow fields and abandoned lots around town and identify what's growing. Plenty of so-called weeds are actually native plants that are useful as edibles or just downright pretty. If it can spring up through cracks in concrete, it can thrive in your garden.

## Sunny and Wet

* Blue flag iris (*Iris versicolor*)
* Cardinal flower (*Lobelia cardinalis*)
* Indian paintbrush (*Castilleja* species)
* Ironweed (*Vernonia* species)
* Joe Pye weed (*Eupatorium* species)
* Marsh marigold (*Caltha palustris*)
* Pussy willow (*Salix discolor*)

## Shady and Wet

* Horsetail (*Equisetum* species)
* Labrador violet (*Viola labradorica*)
* *Ligularia stenocephala* 'The Rocket'
* Ostrich fern (*Matteuccia struthiopteris*)
* Siberian iris (*Iris siberica*)

*Ligularia stenocephala*

# PLANNING AND DESIGN

Now that you've considered the pros and cons of your gardening space, it's time to get started planning your garden. This is your opportunity to bust out and get creative. It's fun to pore through magazines and daydream about creating a masterpiece, but when it comes down to it, don't let all that hype about popular trends and keeping up with the Joneses cramp your style. If your dream is a thousand pink flamingos set against a backdrop of magnificent cactus dahlias, then by all means go for it. Your garden is your mini wonderland and should be a reflection of who you are, not who you think you should be.

## WHO ARE YOU?

What kind of garden makes sense for you? The key to a successful garden begins with working within the boundaries of your lifestyle and experience. Knowing when you garden and what your schedule will permit will prevent disaster later. One of the biggest mistakes a gardener can make is overplanting in the early days of the growing season when plants are small, water is abundant, and enthusiasm is high. You're on fire and unstoppable now, but, when the summer heat kicks up and all those cute little seedlings grow up, the workload can increase exponentially. Before planting that flat of seeds decide how much garden you can handle.

### Growing Under a Tree

In early spring, deciduous trees are still leafless, which allows plenty of light through to reach early blooming perennials, ground covers, and flowering bulbs. Take advantage of precious real estate under trees and grow a ton of pretty flowers. Most of these will spread and naturalize over the years, creating a stunning tidal wave of color.

* Crocus
* Cyclamen
* Forget-me-not (*Myosotis* species)
* Grape hyacinth (*Muscari* species)
* Primrose
* *Tulipa tarda*
* Scilla
* Species tulips
* Snowdrops (*Galanthus* species)

## Ask yourself the following questions:

* How much time do I have to commit to my garden?
* Will I be gardening in the ground or in containers only?
* When do I plan to garden? Mornings? Nights? Weekends only?
* How often do I go away on vacation for two days or more?
* How big is my space?
* When and how will I use the garden?

If this is your first time gardening, start small. Gardening should be fun, not a cumbersome chore or a second job. Once you've got some experience under your belt, you'll have a better gauge of how much is too much and how much is just right.

## KNOW YOUR PLANTS

Six-inch potted plants all look kind of the same at the garden center. But they have a way of morphing into something unexpected in the garden. What seems small and manageable can easily grow into an unruly beast. When planning your garden, get to know key facts about coveted plants beforehand. Check out a good plant identification book from the library, read plant tags, and consult with garden center employees if you're unsure about a specific plant.

## Ask yourself about:

* What is its growing habit? Is it bushing, trailing, climbing, or tall and upright?
* How tall will it get? Place that 5-foot behemoth behind smaller, compact plants.
* When does it flower? Plan your garden to evolve with the seasons. Don't pack all the excitement into a short month of flowers followed by several months of boring.
* What kind of conditions does it prefer? Does it need lots of light or plenty of shade? Does it prefer wet soil or a chance to dry out? Plants that aren't suited to the conditions of your garden will only make more work or will die within a few months.
* How much care will it need? Nix the fussy plants. One or two are manageable, but a garden full of needy nellies that require a ton of care and specialized attention will suck the life out of you in no time.

## Finding Inspiration

Inspiration for creative garden ideas lurks in unlikely places. You can create gardens around themes such as your favorite color, smells, vacation spots, plant types, your favorite food (Mexican, pasta ingredients), or your favorite book. You can grow a Gothic garden with all-black flowers or flowers that only bloom at night.

Of course your garden doesn't require a cohesive theme. You can plan it around what you want to look at when you drink your morning coffee or based on more random reasons. One clever YouGrowGirl.com contributor had her dog design her garden for her. Each day her dog ran the same trail through the grass and weeds in her yard so she dug garden beds in the spaces between the pathways her dog had carved out for her.

# GARDENING WITH YOUR COMPUTER

Computers can enhance your gardening experience, especially when it comes to planning, finding inspiration, and researching solutions. The Internet is an invaluable resource for seeds, plants, and information, as well as an incredible connection to legions of like-minded gardening guys and gals. Following the blogs of gardeners from around the world is both eye-opening (you're not the only one who kills a plant now and again) and inspiring. I've been keeping an online journal on **YouGrowGirl.com** for years and find it very useful for keeping a record of what has come and gone in my garden, what worked, what didn't work, and what happened when. I've put out virtual calls for help in the forum at **YouGrow Girl.com** and received an avalanche of useful answers.

If you get your kicks in the designing and planning stage, all kinds of software packages are available that will assist your obsessive urge to arrange and plan before getting into the dirt. Some programs come equipped with tiny plant diagrams that can be manipulated and organized around a scaled grid of your garden space.

Other packages have been designed for the absentminded, neglectful, or, face it, downright anal gardener. These programs prepare an organized database of your plants and their care needs. The software will actually remind you when to water or fertilize specific plants and indicate exactly how much water or food to give them!

## Keeping an Online Journal

Keeping an online journal is a simple and thorough way to chronicle your gardening experience. As a bonus, others can join in, offering their own advice and experiences. It's an easy, high-tech way to meet gardening soul sisters, as well as to share tips and inspiration. The best part is that you can compare notes with other gardeners growing within the same climate or city. I also follow the activities of gardeners growing in vastly different climates via the **YouGrowGirl.com** journals and admit to some serious envy of the exotic plants and longer growing season enjoyed by southern gardeners. The grass is always greener.

Online gardening journals are becoming quite popular—a new batch seems to crop up every spring. To find other like-minded bloggers, type "garden blog" or "garden journal" into a search engine. Or go to **YouGrowGirl.com** and check out the online journals and dive into the forums.

Creating your own journal is as easy or complex as you can handle—find a service that sets you up with an easy-to-use template, join a group weblog, or code your own. A digital camera is a useful (but not required) tool that will allow you to show off your skills or help readers figure out what went wrong. The hardest part is finding time to keep it up-to-date! (See Resources section for more information.)

# DESIGNING WITH CONTAINERS

Just about anything, from miniature alpine plants to fruit-bearing fig trees, can be grown in containers as long as you've got the right-sized pot and a place to put it. Being stuck without a patch of soil might seem like a drag, but designing a container garden comes with a lot of benefits. All but the largest containers are easily portable and can be moved on a whim to fill empty spaces, soften rough edges, and add instant charm. If you become bored with your garden or something just isn't working right, rearranging a few containers is a lot easier than digging up an entire garden. Containers aren't just vessels for holding soil but a key part of the design—and since they come in a wide assortment of colors, shapes, and sizes, your possibilities are endless.

There's no need to limit your use of containers to hard surfaces and decks. A container placed in a particularly bland area of the garden becomes the star attraction. Colorful pots bursting with flowers can be stuck right into the garden, while cascading plants actually look better growing over the edge of a container than lying flat on the ground.

## CLASS FROM CRAP

Anything with sides deep enough to hold soil can be altered to hold a plant, even if only temporarily. Liberate empty drawers, olive oil cans, and thrift store "junk" into functional, innovative containers for planting. Old junk makes stylish, totally original containers that you won't find at your local department store. Get creative with a child's wagon that's busted, old boots, a teapot, or a watering can. It sounds hippieish, but with the right attitude you can make any container cool. The key is to drill drainage holes in the bottom before putting in the plants (see next page for instructions) and to think about how much watering each container might need. If you're unsure about the stability of a particular pot, line it with plastic to hold in soil and protect it from water damage. Poke a few holes in the bottom of the liner for drainage if you can.

Stylish junk can also be turned into platforms to raise containers up off the patio. Eclectic containers look better when they're displayed at staggered heights than when on the same plane. Broken chairs, stools, small tables, and upside-down containers rescued from the trash add dimension to low-rise pots or planted wine crates. Even really junky trash like cinder blocks, bricks, and large rocks can come in handy.

## Stale Ale

Pots with that mossy old patina are where it's at. Make use of that post-party, bottom-of-the-bottle beer or back-of-the-fridge yogurt to grow aged-looking moss on terra-cotta pots.

**1.** Using a paintbrush or sponge, generously paint either beer or yogurt on the sides of unglazed containers that have that drab "new" look.

**2.** Rub soil from the garden on top of the painted-on beer or yogurt. Better yet, if you have access to some moss, sprinkle little pieces onto the treated surface.

**3.** Fill the pots with moistened potting soil or grow a moisture-loving plant such as African violet in the pot. This will keep the pot moist throughout the process.

**4.** Place the painted pots in a shady location. In a few months, gorgeous green moss will grow on the pots!

## PREPARING USED POTS

Thrift stores, flea markets, garage sales, and auctions are great places to get good quality, unusual terra-cotta or ceramic pots without busting your budget. Look for rad vintage containers from the 1950s and 1960s shaped like bunnies and elephants or printed with futuristic atomic patterns.

All used pots, regardless of type, will need to be cleaned and sterilized before use. Old pots can harbor plant diseases left by their former inhabitants. Spreading them to your healthy plants would be a drag. Instead, soak newly purchased finds in a solution of 1 part bleach or hydrogen peroxide (aka oxygenated bleach) and 10 parts warm water. Scrub the pots with a soft brush to remove hard mineral buildup, rinse thoroughly, and set on a dish rack or towel to dry.

It's a bummer, but most vintage pots and bowls were made without drainage holes. If you'd rather keep your objet d'art intact, place a layer of gravel or broken pot shards in the bottom of the container before filling it with soil. An inch or two should do, depending on the depth of the container. This will keep your plants from drowning, but be careful when you water not to overdo it. Drilling drainage holes is best for long-term growing, and can easily be done using an electric drill and a ½-inch bit. A masonry or ceramic bit is necessary to push through hard terra-cotta and ceramic. Get geared up with protective gloves and eyewear before you start the procedure. Turn the pot upside down and drill one or more holes into the bottom depending on the size of the pot. Be patient and don't push too hard or you'll cause a crack. Stop and let the bit cool if things get too hot.

## MEDIUM COOL

I admit that I have a shallow, vain side—reach for the best-looking containers first. C'mon, good-looking containers make good-looking gardens! Of course, like all things in life, function is just as important as style. When choosing a container, consider how the material it is made from will serve both your needs and the needs of your plant over the long term.

### Terra-cotta and Clay

Pros:
Classy shapes and designs. Porous material is great for drought-tolerant plants.

Cons:
Crack and break if left outside in freezing temperatures. Soil dries quickly, making them a poor choice for hot decks or starting seeds. Large containers are heavy to lift or move.

### Pool Garden

Transform a plastic kiddie pool into a groovy herbal oasis fit for a deck or rooftop space. Ask your landlord or consult with a contractor or builder friend to be sure your rooftop deck can handle the weight beforehand. Drill or puncture lots and lots of holes (at least one hole for every 6 square inches of space) into the bottom of your pool for drainage. Prop the pool on top of old bricks so water can flow from underneath. Fill the pool with potting soil and plant it with shallow-rooted flowering herbs, drought-resistant plants, or ornamental grasses. Now, that's class.

## Plastic

Pros:

Lightweight. Holds moisture well. Great for seed starting. Easy to clean. Can stay outside all year.

Cons:

Ugly designs, cheap looking. Can hold water too well, making it a poor choice for drought-loving plants. May fade in bright light.

## Galvanized Metal

Pros:

Gorgeous! Find cheap buckets at hardware and farm supply stores. Won't rust.

Cons:

Absorbs heat on hot decks. Soil dries out faster. Usually need to pierce holes for drainage.

## Wood

Pros:

Has a natural, warm aesthetic. Wood breathes, and your plants like that. Can be affordable if the wood is reclaimed.

Cons:

Can rot (unless you use a naturally rot-resistant wood such as cedar). Expensive if bought new.

## Tin Cans

Pros:

Cheap or free! Look cool.

Cons:

They rust.

## Gussy Up Your Cheap Containers

Here's a cool way to turn boring plantings into art. Sink cool, vintage swizzle sticks into the soil until only the decorative top part is showing. Or create simple or complex scenes (dioramas) with plastic figurines and dollhouse and train set miniatures. Pretend an old smashed-up toy car has been crushed by the "trunk" of a topiary geranium. Mix figurines and plants that work to scale. Mosses such as Irish moss make fabulous faux grass.

# PLANTER BOX

On a sunny rooftop deck, wooden planter boxes are the best places to grow large plants. But a simple, no-fuss planter box is difficult to find. This project is perfect for anyone who can drill a hole and turn a screw.

Modify the design to make your box bigger or smaller to suit your space. Try to find wood that is naturally rot-resistant such as cedar, redwood, black locust, or cypress. This is especially important if you plan to grow edibles in the box. Pressure-treated wood (the stuff with a green hue) is cheaper and lasts longer but is treated with highly toxic chemicals such as arsenic that will leach into the soil and harm your plants. You should also avoid cheaper woods such as pine that are not naturally resistant to rot. Before you know it, your box will be warped and falling apart, whereas a cedar box will last several years.

## You Will Need

* Cedar or other naturally rot-resistant wood (see cutting list below for amounts)
* 1½-inch decking screws (approximately 68)
* Screwdriver
* Landscaping fabric or plastic sheeting
* Staple gun

# CUTTING LIST

| DESCRIPTION | BOARD SIZE | LENGTH | QUANTITY |
| --- | --- | --- | --- |
| Front and back walls | 1 x 5 | 4 feet | 6 |
| Base boards | 1 x 5 | 4 feet | 3 |
| Side walls | 1 x 5 | 18 inches | 6 |
| Support posts | 2 x 4 | 18 inches | 4 |
| Bottom runners | 2 x 4 | 18¾ inches | 3 |

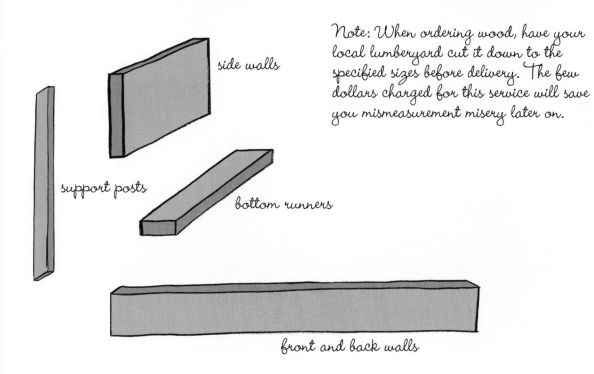

side walls

support posts

bottom runners

front and back walls

Note: When ordering wood, have your local lumberyard cut it down to the specified sizes before delivery. The few dollars charged for this service will save you mismeasurement misery later on.

**1.** Build the base according to the diagram labeled step 1. Evenly space the three baseboards along the bottom runners. These cracks between the pieces will allow for extra drainage and help prevent warping.

**2.** Next build the box shape according to the diagram labeled step 2. Start by screwing a front or side wall board into a support post. Begin by lining up the wall board with the bottom of the support post.

**3.** Continue building all the sides, adding support posts until one row of wall boards forms a complete rectangle (diagram labeled step 3). Once you've got a secure shape, adding a second and third row of boards is easier work.

**4.** When adding your second and third row of wall boards, be sure to space them evenly, leaving gaps between the boards exactly as was done when building the base. These side spaces will also provide drainage and prevent side warping. Before screwing on your third row of boards, check that it is lined up with the top edge of your support posts.

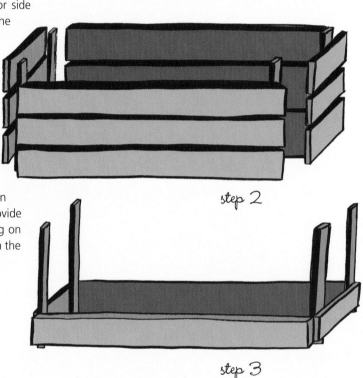

step 1

step 2

step 3

**5.** Flip the base over on top of the box shape. Line it up carefully with all edges and screw the base to the box as indicated in the diagram labeled step 5.

**6.** Have someone help you flip the entire box over and place it in its final position on your deck.

**7.** Unroll the landscaping fabric or plastic sheeting. Starting from the back left corner of your planter box, staple the fabric three quarters of the way down from the top wall board. When the container is filled, the soil will cover this edge and hide the fabric.

**8.** Line the sides and bottom of the planter with fabric. If you use plastic as a lining, poke a few ½-inch drainage holes in the bottom and along the sides.

**9.** Fill your box with good-quality container soil and get planting.

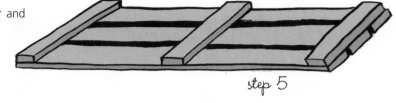

step 5

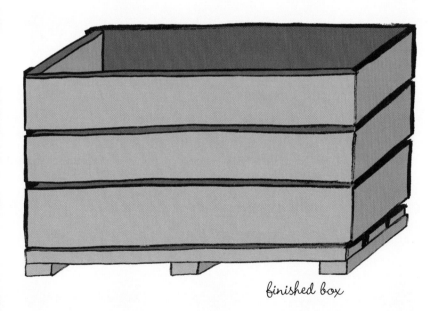

finished box

## Lining Your Box

Both landscaping fabric and plastic sheeting make excellent box liners. Make your choice based on your climate and the type of plants you intend to grow. Landscaping fabric is great in wet climates with a lot of rain. Fabric breathes, allowing excess moisture to evaporate more quickly. However, in hot, dry climates, landscaping fabric allows water to evaporate too quickly. Choose plastic when you want good moisture retention and landscaping fabric when drainage is your primary concern.

# GETTING YOUR FIX WITHOUT GETTING BURNED

Plant shopping is fun, minus that whole money/budget thing. Walking up and down the endless aisles of a garden supercenter is like entering a fantasy land of foliage. The heavens part, a ray of light shines down, the choir sings, and a tear runs down your cheek. Although I know it's very, very wrong, I can't help touching and smelling every single plant I pass regardless of their interest or the care they need. It's an addiction without a twelve-step program. I can't walk past a plant display without stopping and surveying the goods. When I'm in a rush, I still take a moment to take stock quickly from the corner of my eye.

Try to contain yourself in the garden center. They charge a high markup, which can sometimes be worth it because of the quality or selection. But the most popular or common plants can be had for a fraction of the cost elsewhere. Only go into the store with cash if you must—it's far too easy to blow your whole garden budget in one quick shopping spree.

Garden centers are just the tip of the iceberg when it comes to plant acquisition. If your total garden budget is tight, plants are a good place to skimp. Spend a portion of your budget on hard-to-find plants and must-haves, but get the rest through thriftier channels. Here's what I know about getting plants cheap.

* **Buy Off Season**—Fall is a good time to plant perennials, and it is also when lots of garden centers (especially seasonal operations that set up shop in parking lots) are getting rid of stock on the cheap. Some perennials will look a little worse for wear but can easily make a comeback if the damage isn't disease- or pest-related. Choose the best of the lot and prune back the dead parts. Late fall heading into winter is also the perfect time for bargain-bin bulbs, while midsummer is good for seed clearances.

* **Spring Plant Sales**—Churches and horticultural societies are famous for their springtime plant sales. This is when group members donate surplus perennials from their garden to help raise funds for the organization. Plant sales are great because everything is at least half the cost of your typical garden center fare, double the size, and sometimes better cared for. Expect to see a lot of quick-growing or invasive perennials. But hey, you'd pay at least double at your local "Super Plant" for the same thing, so why not?

* **Garden Center Sales**—You don't have to wait until the end of the season to get small discounts at big garden centers. Many wait until the mad mid-spring rush slows down before pulling out small 10 to 25 percent total purchase, one-day sales. My local garden superstore holds Ladies Day every year. No kidding.

* **Garage Sales**—This is where you're likely to find hundreds of spider plant cuttings selling for a buck a pop and little in the way of juicy stuff. But keep your eyes open, 'cause you never know when you'll hit the jackpot.

* **Street and Farmer's Markets**—In my city, the local farmer's market is the cheapest place to get good-quality organic seedlings. Heirloom tomatoes and herbs are the most abundant and popular offerings. I don't bother to grow tomatoes from seed anymore now that I have my yearly farmer's market hookup!

* **Garden Shows**—This isn't the cheapest place to get plants, but since the shows always seem to be held in the dead of winter when I'm foaming at the mouth for some greenery, it's hard to resist. You can usually score a deal or two at these events if you keep your eyes peeled. Some vendors will sell one or two items at rock-bottom prices to lure in customers. Scoop the deal and run before you spy the more expensive eye candy.

* **Trading**—There's nothing like free. I'm a big fan of it. You're guaranteed to get addicted to gardening once you've caught on to a little miracle called propagation—making many plants from one. Take cuttings from your friends' and neighbors' scented geraniums, coleus, herbs, and even tomatoes. Save your seeds at the end of the gardening season and trade the surplus with friends for other coveted varieties. If you're really organized, work out a buddy buying system with a gardener friend. You can plan a group trade in early spring with your gardening pals or your community plotmates. If you're looking for people to trade seeds and cuttings with, go to the forums on **YouGrowGirl.com** and find fellow gardeners who are nearby or just a mailbox away.

* **Online Auctions**—Believe it or not, you can score wicked deals on eBay. If you buy lots of plants or purchase multiple plants from single dealers, you can save on shipping costs. Of course you don't get to see the goods before you purchase, so buyer, beware. To protect yourself, check the seller's rating and read descriptions carefully. Sometimes it's not what's there but what's missing that's important.

* **And All the Rest**—Corner markets and home centers are great places to get plants cheap. Prices range from store to store, of course, so be sure to comparison shop. The thing to keep in mind is that the staff in these places don't have a clue, and that shows in how they care for the plants. "Set 'em and forget 'em" is their philosophy. Try to visit the stores regularly and get plants fresh off the truck. Anything that sits too long might not survive the neglect. This is where real nurseries earn their markup.

*Garden Center Tips*

* Prepare a shopping list first, so you don't go hog wild and blow your budget on cool-looking plants that really won't work in your garden.
* Bring a pocket-sized plant guide with you. You're guaranteed to find one or two or several plants not on your list. A plant guide can help you size up a tempting plant quickly and prevent buyer's remorse.
* Make at least one visit to the garden center as a student rather than a customer. Stores with good selections are a great way to get a feel for plants you've only seen in books.

# WHO TO BRING HOME

It's tempting to pick up every plant in the store that catches your fancy. But hold on—there is so much more to consider besides aesthetics.

## Size It Up

It's a fact—bigger plants cost more money. Some plants are bigger because they actually grow up to become trees and shrubs. Some perennials are larger simply because they've been raised in the nursery a year or two longer than their four-inch-pot counterparts.

Putting mature plants into your garden generates that "well-grown garden" look in an instant, while new garden beds look bare and boring when everything is exactly the same size. Unless you're independently wealthy, you probably can't afford a truckload of big plants. Instead, buy one or two large plants to make an impact and fill the rest of the space with smaller plants that need more time to grow.

## Avoid Prissy Plants

Here today, compost tomorrow. High-maintenance plants sure are pretty, but they take a lot of work and dedication. It will be a terrible blow to your confidence if too many plants die under your watch. Play it safe as a beginner and buy hardy plants that practically take care of themselves. Choose one difficult plant if you absolutely must and work your way up gradually to other finicky plants.

High-maintenance plants are those that are most susceptible to disease or require a lot of extra work at the end of the growing season. Fancy tea roses are a classic example. They need special pruning, lots of fertilizer, and get a whole bunch of difficult diseases.

## Checklist for Choosing a Healthy Plant.

❑ **Check for pests**—Don't forget to look under the leaves where insect pests lurk.

❑ **Choose plants with vibrant leaves**—Stressed-out plants will have yellowing or brown leaves.

❑ **It's in the roots**—Look at the bottom of the pot. If lots of roots are growing out the bottom, the roots have likely gotten twisted up inside the pot while looking for an escape route. This plant has been in the pot too long and has grown its roots into a hard, twisted mass. All that stress can make it difficult for the plant to bounce back after transplanting.

❑ **Size does count**—Choose plants that are short and stocky over tall, thin plants. Plants that are too thin and can't hold themselves up well probably haven't been getting enough light.

❑ **Resist blooming plants**—This is a hard one since it's only natural to reach for the pretty flowers first. Choose plants without flowers (a few unopened buds are cool) and healthy foliage. They'll do better when transplanted because they are putting their energy reserves into making new roots and leaves. Flowers can come later when everything has settled down. Premature flowering is also a sign of unhealthiness. Sick plants put out flowers in a desperate attempt to pass on their genes before they die.

## Checklist for Choosing Bulbs

❏ Avoid bulbs that are too light for their size. This could be a sign of disease.

❏ Do not buy bulbs that are moldy, soft, or shriveled. Healthy bulbs are plump and firm.

❏ Choose the biggest bulbs in the bunch based on variety. Bigger bulbs mean bigger blooms.

## Plants for Where You Are

Choose plants suitable for your climate. If you're in the rainy Pacific Northwest, don't try to grow drought-loving desert plants. Plants not quite adapted to your climate will only make you sweat in the long run. You can bend this rule a little with container plants, but an in-ground garden is susceptible to nature's curveballs.

## Plants That Make an Impact

Every plant follows its own flowering schedule. Some flower once and call it a day, while others keep pumping out the blooms all season long. Choose a few plants that you know will go the extra mile. That way you'll have some flare in the garden when other plants have fizzled. Alternatively, buy a few plants for their foliage instead of their flowering potential. Bold leaf shape, texture, color, or pattern lasts a long time and gives the garden a kick.

# TAG DECODING

You've cruised around the garden center and you're ready to get busy loading your cart with an assortment of glamorous, uncomplicated flora. But first you'll just check the tag. Thunk! That's the sound of your brain smashing into a wall of foreign concepts like "hardiness," USDA zones, and a row of tiny indecipherable icons. This guide will help you to unlock the mysterious language of plant tags.

## THE BASIC MODEL

Most tags carry the bare minimum of information for the consumer. These are the basics:

### Plant Name

This should include the common name as well as the scientific or botanical name. Common names can vary regionally, so the Latin name is there as identification backup.

### Photo

This is handy because it shows you what to expect. Plants are depicted at maturity. At the very least it should show you flower color.

### Lighting

This tells you the ideal lighting situation for the plant. It is either shown as a symbol (a full or half sun icon is popular) or labeled with terms like "sun," "part sun," "part shade," and "shade."

But what exactly do such vague terms mean?

**Full sun**—6 hours of direct sunlight per day.

**Part sun**—4 to 6 hours of direct sun.

**Part shade**—2 to 4 hours of direct sun.

**Shade**—Very little to no direct sunlight. Usually found in woodland areas or underneath large trees. Narrow alleyways are also often shade spots.

### TIP

Don't throw those tags in the trash! Affix them into your garden journal or tuck them into the soil next to the plant. You will undoubtedly forget what you've got a few months down the road. I keep mine in a box, which is a scary reminder of just how many plants I have purchased over the years!

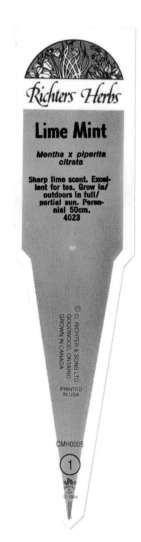

Richters Herbs

**Lime Mint**

Mentha x piperita
citrata

Sharp lime scent. Excellent for tea. Grow in/outdoors in full/partial sun. Perennial 50cm.
4023

© O. RICHTER & SONS LTD.
GOODWOOD, ONTARIO
GROWN IN CANADA

PRINTED
IN USA

CMH0005

1

# Size

Usually shown in both inches and centimeters, this key information lays out the size your plant is expected to reach at maturity. Size often indicates height and sometimes includes spread (how wide your plant will grow). Be sure to check this information when considering a plant. Bring a ruler along if you need something to give an accurate idea. That globe thistle sure did look tiny in the pot, but wait until next year when it has taken over half the garden.

## THE DELUXE MODEL

Some plant tags go the extra distance, providing detailed, helpful information. If you see a tag with this much info, you're rockin'.

# Location/Moisture

This category is more involved than exposure, getting into specifics about the preferred soil type for your plant. It might also tell you how much water the plant needs and whether it can withstand drought or prefers boggy soil. Examples include "Average to moist, well drained soil," or "Prefers dry conditions."

# Flowering Time

Indicates the months of the year your plant is most likely to bloom and put on a show, i.e., "Blooms all summer" or "Small white flowers in late spring."

# Spacing

Spacing prevents you from creating a crowded, unhappy mess by explaining the distance this plant should be placed from others in the garden. This is often indicated on the tag with the phrase "Plant 12 inches apart," or with arrows pointing left and right to indicate width between plants.

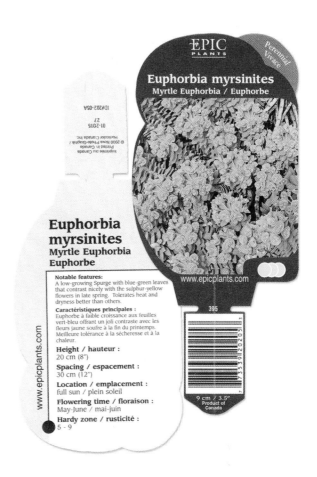

# Special Features/Use

Tags bearing this type of information are downright fancy! Incudes info such as whether or not the plant can be used for eating or cut flowers, if it attracts butterflies or hummingbirds, and whether you've got a high-maintenance or an easy-grow plant on your hands.

# ANNUALS, BIENNIALS, PERENNIALS

Not all plants are created equal. Each has its own schedule and predetermined growth cycle. Knowing which plant does what will help you decide what to buy and where to put it once you've got it.

## Annuals

Annuals are flowering plants that do their duty in one growing season before becoming compost. This tends to make them the showgirls of the flowering world, doing it up like nobody's business before the lights go out. Annuals seem to flip from popular to passé every year, but they're mighty handy in a start-up garden. Perennials will last for years, growing big and brilliant, but they can take a few years to come into their own. Until then, annuals make good space fillers—they grow fast and put on a show with minimal fuss. Buy a few but don't commit an entire garden to them. An annual garden is bare next spring (self-seeders excluded), forcing you to start fresh every year. Self-seeding annuals drop an abundance of seeds in the fall, which leap into action all by themselves come spring. Self-seeders such as annual poppies and snapdragons come back with a vengeance every year, which makes them seem like perennials when in fact they are not.

## Biennials

There really isn't much advantage to biennial plants. They're a botanical tease: the first year is spent making foliage before flowers appear the second year. Then the show is over and you're back to square one.

## Perennials

Perennials go the distance, coming back for more every year, often bigger and badder than ever. They cost a few dollars more than an annual, but once they're in the ground they're there for the long haul. Plus you can divide them up and trade for new plants when they get too big. Unfortunately, they can take a few years to become something great. It was three years before my perennial garden made the transition from interesting to awesome. But it's worth the wait!

# PLANT SCIENCE

Most plants have two names: a common name and a scientific (Latin) name. Using Latin names sounds nerdy and pretentious, especially when common names are so easy, but it's actually a valuable communication tool that will make asking questions at the nursery and talking to other gardeners a whole lot clearer. Plus, it makes you feel really smart.

Here's the deal: the same plant can have multiple common names, and the same common name can be used to describe lots of different plants depending on whom you're talking to and where you're from. Scientific names are a common language anyone can use, effectively breaking language barriers. A gardener in Japan may not know a poppy from popcorn, but when you say *Papaver somniferum,* everyone's on the same page.

What you should know: A plant's Latin name (also known as "botanical name") is a two-part system that works like a superhero decoder ring to give you information about what a plant looks like. The first word indicates the genus (or group) the plant belongs to. All plants that begin with this name share common characteristics. The second name, the species, further places the plant into another category based on shared similarities. When you start to identify plants with the same genus name, it all begins to make sense. For instance, tomatillo, cape gooseberry, and Chinese lantern are plants that all share the genus name *Physalis*, and each bears fruit that is encased in a distinctive papery husk.

Don't pressure yourself to memorize and recite scientific names like you're cramming for a national spelling bee. This kind of learning can happen gradually over time. You'll be surprised by how much seeps in naturally just by looking at tags and talking to other gardeners.

# PLANT

You've got your master plan for total garden domination and a tray of super plants at the ready, so now what? Figuring out this whole soil thing and then getting your babies in there alive may seem intimidating, but with a few easy instructions and a bit of practice it will all become second nature.

While springtime is the traditional planting season, you can get to planting at just about any time of the year unless the ground is frozen solid or the sun is scorching hot. Adjusting to new digs is hard work for plants when conditions are on either end of extreme, but autumn and spring are ideal times in most zones.

Whatever your part of the world, aim for a period of mild weather when the soil is moist, but not flooding. Hurricane season is not a good time! Days of light rain are actually great for planting if you can stand getting a little wet, and they save you the effort of lugging out the hose or heavy buckets of water. My motto is "Let nature do the work, I'm going inside to watch a DVD."

This chapter breaks down the ins and outs of getting your garden and soil good and ready for planting, growing seedlings, and actually getting plants into the ground or container. The secrets behind soil ingredients, mulches, and amenders are revealed to take the guesswork out of shopping for necessities. And of course to balance out the dulls, there are creative sewing and building projects so handy gals can get their craft on.

# SOILED AGAIN

When you think about dirt, you probably think about getting stains on your new white jeans, not "Wow, soil is a complex living organism!" But soil *is* a complex living organism, teeming with life and nutrients. This is the stuff that literally grows your plants. Soil is so important to the life of the plant that most organic gardeners consider gardening really to be about growing the soil.

Different plants need different types of soil, and every patch of dirt is different. Before plopping a plant into the ground, first consider what you've got and what you'll need to improve it. Get up close and personal with your dirt. Find out what's in it, what it feels like, and even what it tastes like! Knowing your soil can mean the difference between a happy garden and a wilting garden. Growing plants that suit your soil is way easier than changing your soil to suit your plants.

## ALL ABOUT pH

A two-minute science lesson:

All soil exists on a scale between highly acidic (pH of zero—battery acid) and highly alkaline (pH of fourteen—lye). And right in the middle is seven (archival paper, bottled water). The pH affects how easily your plant can absorb nutrients. Neutral soil is an ideal environment for good bacteria to carry out the decomposition process. Most plants prefer a neutral soil because it allows the most nutrient absorption, but some specialized plants require a pH just up or down from neutral. Generally, soil that measures above seven may be too alkaline for most plants but perfect for clematis, peony, peas and beans, or saxifrage. On the flip side, soil that measures below six is terrific for acid lovers such as blueberry, azalea, rhododendron, heather, or bog plants, but it's a nightmare for a vast majority of popular garden plants.

### Acid Test

You can easily figure out the pH of your soil yourself using a home test kit that you can get cheap at the garden store. A quicker but more expensive option is to buy a meter with a soil probe that gives readings on contact. Or, if you are having your soil tested at a lab for other issues like nutritional deficiencies and pollutants, have them check your soil pH at the same time.

When testing, be sure to take several readings from various parts of the garden. The pH can actually shift from place to place, so it is best to find out what is happening all over your space and average it out.

To use a simple home pH test kit, mix a soil sample with neutral-pH distilled water. Your next step will depend on the type of testing kit. You will either mix your sample with a special powder, or dip a strip of testing paper into it. Both kit types create a reaction with the soil that produces a new color. Match the resulting color against the chart that is provided to determine the pH of your soil.

### Altering pH

Generally speaking, altering the natural pH of your garden is an uphill battle involving the never-ending addition of costly soil amenders. You can make things easier by accepting what you've got and planting accordingly rather than struggling to overhaul your soil to suit the needs of one coveted plant. If you absolutely must have that blueberry patch or azalea garden, here's how to go about shifting soil pH.

**Neutralizing Soil**—If your soil is on the high side of alkaline or acidic, you can bring it closer to a neutral pH gradually with the addition of organic matter such as compost. As organic matter builds in your soil, the nutrients in the soil will also build, shifting the pH away from the extremes.

**Acidifying Soil**—Sulphur is the most common amender for quickly boosting your soil's acidity. You can buy garden sulphur (aka elemental sulphur) at the garden store. Get the granular kind—the powder version will get in your nose and eyes if you don't wear protective gear.

Other easy-to-find amenders that will raise the acidity of your soil at a slower pace include peat, pine needles, black tea leaves, or coffee grounds. Mix some into your soil before planting acid-loving plants and cover with a layer of mulch. You can also give your plants a daily drink of cold tea or leftover coffee.

**Alkalinizing Soil**—Limestone or crushed oyster shells will raise the pH of your soil to a more alkaline level. Limestone comes in two forms: dolomitic lime or calcitic lime. The type that is right for your garden depends on how much magnesium is present in your soil. Of course this will necessitate another test to determine the soil's nutritional content. This is all such a big pain that it's really better to just grow plants suitable for your soil and skip the confusing mess.

## NUTRIENTS AND DEFICIENCIES

Just as eating health food instead of junk food produces happy, healthy people, happy, nutrient-rich soil will produce happy, healthy plants. The nutritional value of soil comes from a variety of ingredients, but primarily, we're talking phosphorus, nitrogen, potassium, calcium, and magnesium.

Unfortunately, not every garden is blessed with gorgeous, rich earth. Before attempting to build your dirt, it's a good idea to do a simple test that will determine what you're lacking. As with pH testing, you can get a home test kit for cheap at the garden store. For a big blast of info about your soil, send your dirt to a soil testing lab (see Resources). For the most accurate result, take samples from multiple spots in your garden at a variety of soil depths. Don't just scrape a bit off the surface!

### Reading Weeds

Sure, you've probably come to despise weeds that seem to plague your glamorous gardening life, but many weeds can provide a useful service as soil signposts. Certain weeds, called indicators, thrive in specific types of soil. Take note of which weeds seem cozy in your garden, especially those that persist in abundance, and refer to this chart to find out what they have to say about your soil.

| INDICATES | PLANTS |
| --- | --- |
| Alkaline soil | Bladder campion, sow thistle, henbane, mustard |
| Acidic soil | Red sorrel, dandelion, bracken fern, oxeye daisy |
| Compacted soil | Bindweed, chicory, quackgrass, wild mustard, knotweed, goosegrass, pineapple weed |
| Poorly drained soil | Horsetail, ground ivy, yellow nutsedge |
| High fertility | Purslane, mallow, chickweed, lamb's quarters, red clover, stinging nettle |
| Low fertility | Plaintain, daisy, wild carrot, mullein, red sorrel, yarrow |

### Eat Dirt

Way back when, it was common for gardeners to test the pH of their soil by tasting it. Alkaline soil is often referred to as sweet because it has a slight sweet taste on the tongue, while acidic soil is referred to as sour or bitter for obvious reasons.

*plantain*

*lamb's quarters*

# TEXTURE

When thinking about the texture of your soil, imagine it as particles. Soil is made up of zillions of them—some big, coarse, and gritty, some tiny and soft. Most soils will fall into one of three main texture categories based on particle size: sand has the largest particles, followed by silt, and clay is the baby bear. The larger the particles, the more freely air and water will move through them, which affects the type of plants you can grow.

## Sand

Sandy soils are fast-draining, meaning water moves through them quickly. This type of soil is great for lots of different types of cacti and succulents but is also found in some marshy areas. Another advantage to sandy soil is that it heats up quickly. Unfortunately, sandy soils often lack nutrients, and the fast drainage means that any nutrients that are present quickly drain away.

If your garden is heavy on the sand, try adding some organic matter to it. Chopped-up leaves and compost will lighten it up and provide a nutrient boost.

## Silt

Silt is like clay lite. It has the disadvantages of clay (see below) but to a slightly smaller degree. The result is a soil that is cool and silky when wet, crumbly and dusty when dry. Unfortunately it is slightly less nutrient-rich than clay.

## Clay

That sticky, malleable stuff you used to make ashtrays in kindergarten is clay, and (guess what?) clay comes from the ground. Cross your fingers it's not in your backyard. Generally clay earth is great for sculpture class but a waking nightmare as garden soil. Clay soil can be hard and compact when dry, sticky and cold when wet, and is a real back-breaker to dig up. It holds water tightly with little room for air movement, promoting root rot in some plants. The good news is

that the small particles also hold nutrients well, and some plants really like a waterlogged environment.

Add lots and lots of organic matter and sand to clay soils to break up that fine texture. Add organics such as compost or leaf mold until you can't add any more—and then add some more. I'm going to give it to you straight: altering a clay bed is a lot of work that takes some patience. If you don't have it in you, try embracing the clay and grow plants that like wet feet such as dogwood bushes (*Cornus*), ostrich fern (*Matteuccia struthiopteris*), southern blue flag iris (*Iris virginica*), astilbe, and ligularia.

## Loam

Loam is soil made up of fairly equal portions of sand, silt, and clay, plus a healthy portion of decomposed organic matter. It's not too hard when dry, not too slick when wet, but just right. Loam is coveted as the ideal soil type because it provides perfect growing conditions for a wide range of plants. It kind of looks and feels like Black Forest cake, but sadly does not taste like it!

## TEXTURE TESTS

Check your soil texture with these simple methods:

### Hands On

Scoop up some soil in your hand. Mush it between your fingers, look at it, even taste it if you're feeling adventurous (watch out for inedibles). Sandy soils should feel gritty, silt feels silky and almost soapy, while clay feels sticky. Now squeeze the soil with your hand. If it forms a tight shape you've got a high concentration of clay; if it crumbles it's sand.

### Water Soak Test

**1.** Mix 1 cup of soil sample and 1 tablespoon of dishwashing powder in a jar.

**2.** Fill the jar with water, screw on the lid, and shake vigorously for several minutes.

**3.** Set the jar aside to allow the layers to settle. They will actually settle in order of weight based on particle size, with sand falling first, silt second, and finally clay. It can take up to a few days for clay to settle into place.

Once the layers settle, measure them with a ruler. If the layers are fairly equal, congratulations, you've got loam. Well-draining, nutrient-rich loam is the ideal soil type most gardeners covet and strive to attain!

## MAKING GOOD DIRT

Plants suck a lot of nutrients out of any soil. Even if you have dreamy, rich loam, you'll need to add nutrients to make up for what your plants continuously deplete. You can bring soil back up to snuff by adding nutrient-rich organic matter every spring and fall. The quick-and-dirty method is to lightly scratch compost or other appropriate amenders into the soil surface. All the goodness will make its way into the soil over time.

mush the soil between your fingers

squeeze the soil with your hand

does it form a shape?

## Compost

Compost is the best soil amender around. Gardeners don't call it "black gold" for nothing. Use it to build up nutrients, improve drainage, and achieve that loamy humus we all desire. The best part is, it's free! You can make your own compost using leftover kitchen scraps and garden waste. It's the ultimate recycling program, since everything that is taken out of the soil can be put back in with compost.

Making compost is easy; finding space for a composter is not. Gardeners with small yards can bury scraps between rows in the veggie plot or underneath trees. You can even make a small compost bin for a rooftop deck (see page 50).

## Mushroom Compost

Mushroom compost is a by-product of the commercial mushroom farming industry. The bags sold at garden centers contain used compost that is no longer useful to the mushroom grower but great for the gardener. It's a mix of manure, either peat or grasses (like straw), and a grab bag of other nutritional elements. It is quite light and has some nutritional value—a good addition to compacted soil.

## Manure

Ah, the goodness of poo! When properly aged, animal manure is a terrific source of nitrogen, organic matter, and other trace elements. Do not add fresh manure to your garden—it stinks, often contains weed seeds and pathogens, and can burn plants. Instead, throw it in the compost bin or age it for six months. If you're crazy enough, scoop up the roadside manure left by police horses. How do you like them apples?

## Leaves

Leaves are another fabulous (and totally free) source of organic matter. Collect leaves from your yard, your neighbors' yards, or anywhere you can find them. Leaves can be left where they drop as mulch or shredded before applying to your garden. Lawn mowers and weed whackers double as leaf-shredding machines that will accelerate the decaying process. To shred with a mower, mow over fallen leaves right on the lawn before collecting with a rake. To shred with a handheld weed whacker, fill a garbage bin with leaves and hack away. Another option is to compost your leaves to produce leaf mold, a highly nutritious humus material that is great for adding nutritional content to sandy soil and for lightening clay. If you don't have a compost bin, stash a plastic bag filled with leaves in an out-of-the-way location for a year or more to allow decomposition to take place. Poke a few holes in the bag to provide air. Watch out for walnut leaves, which contain a chemical that is toxic to some plants.

## Peat

Forget what those other gardening books say, it turns out that peat moss is not the best soil additive. It is light, fluffy, and seems ripe as a quick fix for hard soil. However, its high acidity makes it a bad choice for maintaining a neutral environment (but great for blueberries and other acid-loving plants). While a giant bale of peat won't break the bank, it can be costly over the long term because it sinks into the soil, requiring you to add more continuously. But the real reason to stay away from peat is because it's native to rare wetland environments such as fens and bogs. These natural habitats are slowly being destroyed as they are "mined" to provide peat for use in the gardening industry. If you must have peat, try a substitute such as coir (see below).

## Coir

Coir is becoming the hot peat substitute. It is made from the hairy outer layer of coconut shells and is similar to peat in weight, texture, and acidity. The trouble with coir is that it has no nutritional value, so you'll need to back it up with some compost.

## Getting It Cheap

Compost, leaves, and even manure can often be had on the cheap or even free! You can build or buy a bin and make your own compost in your yard or on your deck or fire escape (see page 50). If you have even less space, you can make an under-the-sink vermicomposter (see page 95) or fashion a small compost bin from a plastic container. You can contact your city and see if they have municipal compost—it's not as clean and chemical-free as what you'd make yourself, but it'll do the job.

Collect leaves from your lawn or ask neighbors if you can have theirs—if you're willing to rake them up, you'll probably get more than you know what to do with. You can let someone else do the dirty work by grabbing bags of leaves left for curbside pickup.

Farms, police horse stables, and zoos are good cheap sources of manure. Be sure to compost it for at least 6 months!

# MAKING COMPOST

Compost is the cycle of life in action: plants decompose and provide nutrition for new plants. Making your own compost is a satisfying process that is easily done by setting scraps and plant waste aside to rot. While there are many methods, some of which are complex or require space, the best bet for gardeners who are short on space and long on time is a cold compost method done in a container or garbage can. In no time you'll have a nice pile of nutritious black gold to add to your garden.

**1.** The first thing to do is collect a mix of dry browns and wet greens (see box). It is best to have more dry material to balance out the wet.

**2.** Put a 6-inch layer of browns in the hole/bin/pile followed by a 2- to 4-inch layer of greens. Repeat.

**3.** Sprinkle the pile with water. Compost ingredients should be on the damp side but definitely not soaking in it!

**4.** Cover the pile with lots of dirt or close the lid of your container. After a few days or a few weeks check on your pile (hole-dug piles can be left alone). Toss your ingredients around with a pitchfork or shovel. This is called **aerating**, and compost needs air to really get rocking.

**5.** The length of time it takes to produce compost depends on the size of the pile, the size of the ingredients added, and the amount of heat generated. Cold piles can take as long as a year to decompose. Check your pile every other week to aerate, water, and monitor progress.

**6.** You can also add food scraps from the kitchen on a regular basis. To do this, bury the scraps inside the pile. Don't just place them on top where they won't get much microbial action.

**7.** You'll know your pile is done when you're left with lovely black, earthy-smelling humus. Add it to your garden or make compost tea and bask in the glory of your accomplishment!

## What You'll Need

Find a good place to make the magic happen. This can be a large pile, a wooden box, a hole in the ground, a special bin, or a container filled with worms. Compost can happen anywhere, so don't be concerned about buying a fancy container.

The following ingredients are ideal for your pile. Whatever you do, do not add oil, meat scraps, fat, or bones. These ingredients will stink up a cold pile, attract all kinds of rodents, and antagonize your neighbors.

\***Browns (Dry, Carbon-rich):** Dry leaves, dry grass, newspaper, dead plant clippings, wood branches, hay, straw, nut shells.

\***Greens (Wet, Nitrogen-rich):** Grass clippings, veggie and fruit scraps, coffee grounds, manure, tea bags, fresh leaves, seaweed.

# Troubleshooting

Sometimes compost piles go wrong. You know you've got trouble if your pile has a nasty rotten stink or is just plain not decomposing, period.

* **Smells Like Evil**—Too wet, too much nitrogen, and/or lacking in air circulation. Add more dry browns to the pile, mix it in, and fluff it up.

* **No Action**—Could be too dry and/or overfilled with browns. Add a bit of water, fluff it up to promote good air circulation. If your brown to greens ratio seems off, add some more green kitchen scraps or fresh lawn cuttings.

* **No Critters in the Pile**—Good, healthy compost should attract critters such as worms, slugs, earwigs, and other creepy crawlies. Let them get in there and do their thing.

# MULCH: LOVE IT OR LEAVE IT

Mulch will rock your world! "Mulch" is a strange word for a thick covering of organic or nonorganic matter laid over your garden like a cozy blanket. Mulch keeps the weeds on lockdown, seals in moisture, cools down the soil in the summer, protects plants during winter, and protects soil from hot sun and pelting rain. It also slowly builds the soil and prevents erosion. As an added bonus, mulch can actually attract beneficial insects, such as slug-munching beetles and spiders, to your garden by providing a happy environment for them to take up residence in. Do not underestimate the power of mulch!

Mulching is a nice passive way to improve the nutritional content of your soil, and it looks good, too. For good weed control and soil assistance, be sure to apply mulch at least a few inches deep. It's best to add most mulches while they are wet so they don't suck moisture from the soil. Compost and leaves are perfect mulches because they do double duty as soil amenders and nutrient boosters.

## MULCH-A-RAMA

### Straw

Straw is a useful mulch for all kinds of veggies, including tomatoes. Straw is especially useful because it creates an instant walking path in your veggie plot. If you're into interplanting rather than creating rows, you can simply shift the straw and plant without fuss.

Straw can create a happy habitat for slugs, but it also attracts natural slug predators such as beetles. I say use the straw and let nature duke it out. Be wary of straw (aka hay) that contains an abundance of seed heads, which will unleash a fury of grass seedlings on your garden.

### Pine Needles

Collect pine needles to use as mulch on acid-loving plants like strawberries and blueberries. Pine needles are usually free for the taking from yards with large pine trees, but ask first!

### Plastic

Black plastic is popular as a sheet mulch in the landscaping industry. Black plastic in your garden sounds like a hideous suggestion, but it does a great job warming up the cool spring soil to give you a jump-start on planting tomatoes and other plants that love warm feet. It is also great in a new garden where weed seeds are going wild—no weed can make it through a layer of thick plastic! To disguise the ugliness, I recommend covering it with a layer of bark or straw, or decorative rocks for that groovy-grandma, white-quartz, minimalist look.

### Newspaper

Like plastic, newspaper is a good weed-suppressing sheet cover. It's even better than plastic because you probably already have a pile of it in your recycling bin. Apply a heavy layer of natural mulch on top to keep it from blowing away.

### Grass Clippings

Don't throw away those grass clippings! Grass makes a nitrogen-rich mulch on veggies like tomatoes and peppers. Allow fresh-cut grass to dry out for a few days before applying to the garden since some grasses are so vigorous they could take root and spread.

## Rocks

Rocks, stones, and grit do nothing nutritionally for the soil, but they are great for suppressing weeds, warming the soil, and preventing soil erosion. They come in handy in desert gardens and make a decorative top layer on container-grown cacti and succulents.

## Wood Chips and Bark

Wood chips and bark make a durable, long-lasting mulch that looks great against plant foliage. Wood mulches are made from a variety of wood types, especially cedar and pine. Whatever you do, avoid wood mulch that has been dyed to look like cedar. Not only is the wild color kinda tacky, but it leaches dye into the soil. The word isn't out on whether the dye is dangerous for the garden, but the source of the wood itself—waste wood, sometimes from demolition sites and old shipping palettes—is cause for concern. You should also avoid wood mulches on veggie beds since some woods will poison tomatoes as they decompose. And because wood mulches are slow decomposers, they will actually tie up nitrogen in the soil, making it temporarily unavailable to the plants.

Steer clear of dyed wood chips

## Cocoa Shells

Cocoa shells are the waste product from chocolate factories and sold in any garden center. These deep brown bits are deliciously chocolaty smelling and will make the green in your plants pop. Cocoa shells are acidic in nature and best used on acid-loving gardens. Do not use cocoa in Fido's turf because chocolate is poisonous to dogs.

## Others

Compost, shredded leaves, leaf mold, and seaweed do double duty as nutrient-rich soil amenders and mulch. Lightly scratch them into the soil to aid in the decomposition process.

## Living Mulch

Living mulches are crops that are grown to cover and protect the soil. Farmers grow clover, buckwheat, and alfalfa to protect the soil during winter, add nutritional content, and suppress weeds.

Fast-growing crops of small, early-season plants like salad greens and spinach do double duty as living mulch and dinner. They do excellent work suppressing weeds by taking up space under later-season large plants like tomatoes or corn and let you make the most of your precious garden space.

## To Dig or Not to Dig?

Naturally all this talk about soil will lead to the inevitable question: Should I dig? Rototilling, digging, and double digging are backbreaking labor we'd all like to avoid. Believe it or not, tilling isn't an absolutely necessary chore. Turning over dirt messes with nature's course, sometimes causing more work over the long term. Whether to dig or not is a matter of choice. I personally use a minimal-dig method, digging only when it's necessary to bust up some tough soil, and applying organic matter to the surface otherwise. Let nature get busy and do the work for you.

# CONTAINER PLANTING

Live in an apartment with not much more outdoor space than a fire escape and a windowsill? Or maybe you've got a deck or terrace. Or just a yard your landlord won't let you mess with. Don't sweat it, container gardening might be even better than the real thing. Containers can be moved on a whim, or when you discover that you put a shade-loving plant in the hottest part of your yard. The astonishing truth is that just about anything can be grown in a container. All it takes is a little know-how and experience.

## CHOOSING CONTAINER SOIL

The great thing about container soil is that it's ready to use straight outta the bag. No soil amending or backbreaking digging necessary!

Container-grown plants require a special type of soil referred to as a "soil-less mix" or "substrate." It's technically not soil but a mix of sterile ingredients including peat, sand, vermiculite, or perlite. Whatever you do, do not attempt to grow container plants in soil from your yard. This type of soil will become hard, dry, and compact in a container, promoting root rot and eventually killing your plant. Container-grown plants require good drainage and air circulation—lots of both!

You can buy different container mixes for the different needs of your plants. For example, succulents and cacti are best grown in a formula high in sand and grit and low in organic matter that mimics their natural habitat. Luckily you don't have to worry about special mixes too much because most plants can be grown in a general mix called "potting soil" or "container mix." These light and airy mixes are high in organic content with good water-holding capacity.

As with most things in life, you get what you pay for. Don't buy the cheapest bag of soil on the market. There are other places to save cash, but soil is not one of them! A good rule of thumb to follow when choosing soil is to pick it up and test the weight. Good container soil is light but not too light. Really light soils are full of peat or perlite but lack anything remotely nutritious for the plants. Really heavy soils compact easily, making it impossible for roots to breathe in the pot. Your best bet is to find mixes created for organic growers. These contain some nutritious organic matter, often compost or leaf mold, and sometimes use alternatives to environmentally controversial peat.

# WHAT'S IN CONTAINER MIX

In your early days as a gardener, keep things simple and grab a bag of premixed soil from the garden center. But as you get more advanced, there may come a time when you'd like to try mixing your own container soil. The extra effort is worth it when growing plants with special needs. Or maybe you want to play mad scientist and concoct your own secret formula. All the ingredients can be found at the garden center. Find out what's in the mix and get started.

## Perlite

These large white granules look like tiny bits of popcorn and are actually formed in much the same way by "popping" volcanic ash under high heat. Perlite is a large-sized but very light material that is used to prevent soil compaction and promote good drainage in containers. It is also fairly water absorbent, helping to maintain moisture levels.

## Vermiculite

Vermiculite is a lightweight soil additive derived from the mineral mica. The granules are smaller than perlite but more water absorbent, making it less suitable in containers with cacti or other plants that prefer fast-drying soils.

## Sand

Sand is most often used when growing cacti, succulents, or bog plants. Buy sand that is horticultural grade. Do not collect sand from suspect sources such as golf courses which will inevitably contain high levels of herbicide.

## Peat

Peat is a very common container soil ingredient. While it is very light and airy, it does have a highly acidic pH. As mentioned previously (see Peat, page 49) it is obtained by "mining" marshland and bogs, destroying natural habitat. When possible, use a soilless mix that uses peat substitutes such as coir (see Coir, page 49).

## Moisture Crystals

"Moisture crystals" or "hydrogels" are gel-like substances made from super-absorbent polymers that retain water and hold it in the soil longer. They are promoted as nontoxic, although some hydrogels are derived from synthetic polymers. To be safe, it is best to reserve mixes that contain this ingredient for nonedibles.

## Fertilizer Pellets

Some mixes contain fertilizer pellets that slowly release synthetic fertilizers to the soil as they break down. This type of soil is not recommended if you choose to grow organically. For more on chemical fertilizers, see page 90.

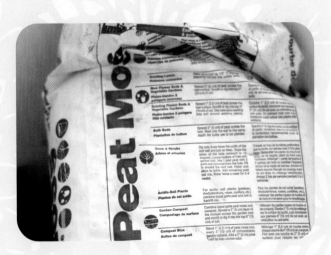

## MULCHING CONTAINERS

Even containers can enjoy the fabulous benefits of mulching—weed control, moisture retention, nutrition, and erosion control. Since containers have a smaller surface area than your average garden, you can be more inventive and indulge in more expensive materials. River stones, marbles, shells, clay pebbles (used in hydroponics), grit, polished glass, beach glass, and bits of slate all make gorgeous, decorative mulches that will also prevent soil erosion when you water, as well as retain heat and moisture. Of course, compost as a mulch is not only free but comes with the added bonus of nutritional value. When adding mulch to containers, avoid piling it up around the crown of the plant where the stem meets the soil. Moisture buildup in that area can rot the stems of some plants.

## GROWING IN CONTAINERS

Just about anything can be grown in containers! All you need to do is choose the right container and take a bit more care. Containers dry out much faster than an in-ground garden, especially when your plants are too big for their pots—the larger the roots, the less room is left in the pot to hold water.

When choosing your plants, remember that some plants grow large root systems requiring room to grow and a lot of water. If you don't think you can make the commitment, choose plants that will stay small and can take a bit of neglect.

Your containers matter, too. Plastic containers may not be the classiest of the bunch, but they hold water well, allowing a bit of leeway when it comes to forgetting to water. Terra-cotta looks fabulous but is very porous and dries out much quicker than plastic. Metal is another good-looking material for containers, but we all know how hot a piece of metal gets on a blazing summer day. Be prepared to get out there more often with the water bucket.

# EDIBLE FLOWER CONTAINER

Make the most of your small space by growing multipurpose plants. This container is easy to maintain, looks gorgeous, and the plants are totally edible. The flowers of most herbs are edible, as are a surprising number of traditional garden flowers. Add some nasturtium flowers to your next salad, spice up vinaigrette with chive blossoms, or make rose geranium ice cream. Impress your friends with cucumber-flavored borage blossoms in a glass of lemonade or candied violas on miniature muffins. Recipes for Chive Blossom–Infused Vinegar and Candied Flowers follow.

## You Will Need

* Window box or pot (minimum 10-inch-wide brim)
* Pot shards or rocks (optional)
* Some well-draining container or potting soil
* Flower seeds or plants

**1.** Place a layer of broken pot shards or rocks in the bottom of your container. This isn't absolutely necessary but can help with drainage and prevent soil from eroding through large drainage holes.

**2.** Fill your container three-quarters full with moistened potting soil. Push some soil off to the sides to create a hole in the middle.

**3.** Gently remove each transplant from its current pot and place it into position in the new container. You can take this time to figure out the arrangement that looks best by moving the plants around in the container. Some plants such as nasturtium can be purchased as transplants or easily grown from seed. If you do plant seeds, leave a healthy space between seeds and plants to compensate for root growth.

**4.** Once you've got the perfect grouping, fill in the spaces around the plants with more soil. Make sure the crowns of your plants (where the root meets the stem) is level with the soil surface. There should be an inch or so of space between the soil and the top of the container.

**5.** Water the plants well.

## Grow Like with Like

Plants grown together in the same container should have similar needs. Grow sun-loving plants that require lots of water together. Don't mix sun and shade or drought-tolerant and bog plants in the same pot—one or both will surely die unhappy.

## Choosing a Style

Smaller pots will hold one plant, but larger containers can be planted with an assortment. The traditional method for grouping plants is to place taller plants toward the back or center, with shorter or trailing plants in front or around the edges. Check your plant tags or seed packets for maximum height info.

# CHIVE BLOSSOM-INFUSED VINEGAR

Chive blossoms make a spicy, aromatic infused vinegar that tastes great on fresh greens or potato salad, or as a marinade. This recipe can also be adapted to create a variety of infusions. Substitute chive flowers with just about any of the flowers listed under Flowers Worth Eating (right). My favorites are African blue basil, lemon basil, sage, and nasturtium flowers.

## You Will Need

* 1 cup chive blossoms
* 1-pint wide-mouth mason jar and non-metal lid
* 2 cups white wine vinegar
* Cheesecloth or fine sieve
* Funnel
* Sterile glass jar

**1.** Wash the chive blossoms quickly under water and pat thoroughly dry with a towel. Salad spinners work well, too. Leave them to air dry for an hour to be sure there is no moisture left.

**2.** Loosely pack the jar half full with the blossoms. Fill the jar to the top with white wine vinegar. The vinegar preserves the flowers, so be sure to cover the chive blossoms completely to prevent mold forming.

**3.** Cover the jar with a plastic or other non-metal lid (metal can corrode) and set in a sunny window where the herbs can steep.

**4.** Carefully shake the jar a few times per week. Over time the blossoms will transform the vinegar to a pretty pink color.

**5.** After 2 weeks, strain the mix through a fine sieve or cheesecloth, being sure to remove all bits of chive debris.

**6.** Using a funnel, pour the vinegar into the fresh jar. You can use a decorative jar or a plain mason jar—the choice is yours.

**7.** Store your jar in a cool dry cupboard away from the sun for up to 6 months.

Makes 2 cups.

## Flowers Worth Eating

* Spicy: Nasturtium, chive blossoms, radish, arugula, dianthus
* Floral sweet: Pansy, viola, chamomile, lavender, lemon verbena, mint, rose-scented geranium, rose, sacred basil
* Fresh: Mint, anise hyssop, borage, lemon basil
* Unusual: Bee balm, calendula, African blue basil, sage, dandelion

# HEALTHIER CANDIED FLOWERS

Candied flowers are most often used for prettying up cakes and other goodies, but if you use fresh flowers grown without chemical sprays, then they are perfectly edible and tasty on their own. Most recipes call for superfine white sugar, but this recipe uses maple sugar—a slightly more health-conscious alternative.

Candy flowers such as pansies, violas, and scented geraniums whole, but pluck and candy individual petals of larger, more complex flowers such as roses.

## You Will Need

* Edible flowers
* Parchment paper
* Egg white
* Small paint brush
* Small, fine-mesh sieve
* Powdered maple sugar

**1.** Lay a flower or petal on a piece of parchment paper and lightly paint it with egg white. The key here is to brush as thin a layer as possible while still covering the entire surface—too much egg white will create a blobby mess.

**2.** Set the first flower aside to dry ever so slightly for 10 to 30 seconds. Go ahead and start on another flower.

**3.** Pour a teaspoon of maple sugar into the mesh sieve. Holding the sieve over the first flower, gently sprinkle a thin layer of sugar over it, being sure to cover the entire surface of the flower.

**4.** Delicately pick up the flower (use a pair of tweezers on smaller flowers) and shake off any excess sugar.

**5.** Set aside to dry on a fresh sheet of parchment or a drying rack and continue with the remaining flowers. Drying can take as long as 24 hours, depending on the humidity.

**6.** Use right away or store in an airtight container.

# GROWING IN A WINDOW BOX

What do you do when outdoor space isn't an option? Try a window box. Contrary to popular belief, window boxes are not just made to hold pansies or a few stringy petunias. Get creative with your window box and turn it into your own miniature high-rise garden.

## TYPES OF WINDOW BOXES

Your average, ready-to-rock store-bought box is available in plastic, terra-cotta, wood, or galvanized metal. Most plastic boxes come in styles such as ugly, boring, and late-1990s hideous. While generally leaning on the bad side of tacky, plastic makes a good water-retaining material for hot, exposed ledges. If you're handy with a screwdriver, have some wood precut at the hardware or lumber store and build your own rectangular box to fit around the plastic form, or simply apply a fresh coat of colorful paint or nail some decorative molding to the front and sides to gussy it up.

If you've got a bit of extra cash to spend, preformed wood, galvanized metal, or decorative terra-cotta boxes are a quick, work-free option. You can also try making window boxes from unexpected items. A 1970s Tupperware container designed to hold celery is the perfect shape for a simple box and a small window. Drill drainage holes using a ½-inch drill bit if necessary. Experiment with rectangular tin boxes, small drawers, and other wood boxes with the tops removed.

*Decorating a Plain Box*
* Wrap it in thick rope.
* Paint it flat or patterned.
* Glue on rocks, bits of broken plate and tile, or shells.

## ATTACHING YOUR WINDOW BOX

A box filled with soil and plants is deceptively heavy. To avoid injury and lawsuits, you'll need to secure your window box to keep it from falling on an unsuspecting pedestrian. How you achieve this depends on your ledge and the material available. The easiest windows are those that have a deep ledge with lots of space to securely hold a window box. I am lucky enough to have such a ledge and have had a small terra-cotta box sitting there for years undisturbed and secure.

Of course, your average window can be much more complicated, but it's still not hopeless! Many city windows have heavy iron bars covering them. These can be utilized to strap or tie the box in place. Ready-made brackets that hold the box will fit over narrow sills and ledges. You can also try screwing directly into a wooden window frame or ledge with long, rust-resistant decking screws. If a brick wall is your only option, you'll need to attach a special heavy-duty bracket to the wall and then attach the box to the bracket. You'll need a masonry bit that can drill through tough brick and mortar. Ask about appropriate materials at your local hardware store to be safe, and, just in case, get permission from your landlord before starting any work on your ledge, especially if it involves drilling or making permanent alterations!

## THE PLANTS

The types of plants that can grow in your box depend on the size of the box and the amount of light and wind it gets. Boxes in full sun will dry out quickly. I recommend filling them with plants that can withstand bright light and short periods of drought. Most cacti and succulents can take some serious dry spells, and so can small clumping grasses such as blue fescue *(Festuca glauca)*. For a contemporary minimal look, try planting an entire box in a single type of grass or succulent. Euphorbias are other minimal-fuss, hardworking sun plants that look really contemporary in a metal box. They come in an assortment of striking leaf colors, from deep purple to silver.

For a drapey, English garden look, try chartreuse or black ipomoea (ornamental sweet potato vine), silver-leafed helichrysum, browny-green bugle *(Ajuga reptans)*, or blue catmint *(Nepeta x faassenii)*.

For a minimal, chic look in the shade, try a box filled with cranesbill *(Geranium macrorrhizum)* or lilyturf *(Liriope muscari)*. For a fuller, draping look, try trailing ivy *(Hedera species)* or *Lobelia erinus*, and try cyclamen or primrose for short growth.

In either sun or shade, you can grow edible flowers (see page 58), herbs, and cooking or salad greens in your box to maximize your use of space. These are especially good for kitchen windows. As you're cooking, just reach and grab what you need! Regular use will promote bushy, healthy growth and keep you in fresh herbs all summer long.

I recommend a mixed box of silver and chartreuse lemon thyme for a fresh-smelling box that will thrive in the sun. In the shade, grow a box filled to overflowing with gorgeous greens. Seek out heirloom lettuce varieties with attractive foliage such as Rouge d'Hiver, red oakleaf, and red velvet. You can even grow baby carrots or lots of luscious strawberries.

## WINDOW BOX TIPS

* Leave some space between the top of the box and the soil line. This will prevent heavy rains or watering from sloshing soil out of the box.
* If long-term care is an issue, attach a planter box as a decorative shell but keep plants in individual pots. That way you can swap dead plants for fresh ones or make changes to suit the seasons.
* To get that full look, stuff your box with lots of plants but be sure to water them well regularly and apply enough fertilizer to make them lush and happy. Remember, the tighter the space, the more often you may need to water.

# GEARING UP

## A GUIDE TO CAN'T-LIVE-WITHOUT-THEM TOOLS

One of the biggest misconceptions about gardening is that you need a lot of tools and contraptions to make the magic happen. In all honesty, you could probably get away with a spoon, fork, paring knife, and pair of scissors if need be. Of course, part of the fun of any hobby or creative endeavor is playing with gadgets and special toys. But what do you really need? The following tools will make gardening easier, more fun, and take you that extra step beyond recycled kitchen utensils without breaking the bank.

### Watering Can

Sure you can use a bucket, or a cup, for that matter. But a big can with a nice big rose attachment (the thing with holes on the end) means the difference between water that splashes onto plants and water that lightly showers them in cool, rainlike sprinkles. Get a good-sized can to avoid running back and forth to the tap. Antique and galvanized metal cans look attractive, but plastic is cheaper, lighter, and more durable. Believe me, after five loads from the tap you'll wish you'd bought plastic.

### Pruning Shears

Pruning shears, cutters, secateurs—whatever they're called, you'll need them. These are going to be one of your best gardening friends, so keep them sharp, oiled, and clean. Secateurs are used for deadheading and clipping branches and dead foliage. There are different types of shears, but the best general-purpose type is called a bypass shear and cuts like a pair of scissors.

Sharp cutters make a clean cut through the plant, but dull cutters rip and tear the plant, encouraging disease. It is really important that you sterilize your cutters after cutting diseased plant foliage to avoid spreading illness from one plant to the next.

## Trowel

Sure, you can use your hands and fingers, but a small handheld trowel will tear through hard clay soil much more effectively, and it's a whole lot easier on your nails. You can find decent used trowels at thrift stores and garage sales. I prefer trowels made from the more durable, rustproof new materials since they tend to take extra wear and tear. You can even get them with softer plastic handles and ergonomic designs.

## Hoe

I've used the term loosely here to cover any tool with this basic shape created for the purpose of hacking into soil and cultivating and loosening the earth. Some hoes have a solid, flat end while others are fork shaped. My personal favorite is a hoe and hook hybrid called the Cobra Head, which was designed and developed by an organic gardener named Noel Valdes. It is a handheld cultivator shaped like, you guessed it, the head of a cobra. It can be used for weeding, digging, and a myriad of other soil-moving jobs.

## Gloves

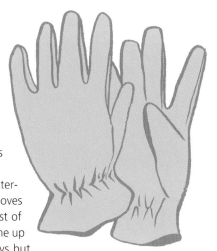

Yes, it can be fun to run your hands through dirt and mulch, but there will be times when gloves come in handy. The best examples are when handling potentially poisonous (poison ivy or oak), prickly (thistles), or contact-sensitive plants. Some people have more extreme contact allergies to plants that have bristly hairs on their leaves and stems. I personally break out in hives just brushing up against sunflowers and cucumber plants.

Cloth gloves breathe well and are washable but are not waterproof and don't provide protection from prickly things. Some gloves are cloth with a rubber coating on the palm, providing the best of both worlds. My personal favorites are fully rubberized and come up halfway to my elbow. They can be a little hot on summer days but provide good protection and can be easily cleaned under the hose.

## Hose

Some of you will not need a hose. Some of you will not have the space or even a hook-up for a hose. But a hose is a handy thing when there's a lot of watering to do and when the heat is on. Apartment dwellers can get smaller, more compact spiral hoses that hook up to standard kitchen or bathroom faucets. A 25-foot hose may just be long enough to wind out the back window and onto the deck on those days when hauling buckets of water is just too much to bear.

## Long-handled Spade

Here's another tool that is essential only for those with yards. Spades are great tools if you've got to dig up a whole lot of earth. It will certainly save you hours on your hands and knees with a small trowel or worse (a kitchen spoon!). Get a spade with a good handle that won't coat your hands in splinters and a tip that won't easily rust or break off on a hard piece of clay.

# CARING FOR YOUR TOOLS

## Clean

After each use, rub or wash off all dirt and debris. Scrape off thick dirt with a piece of plastic or a wire brush. Dry immediately with a rag to prevent rusting.

## Sharpen

Sharpen your tools regularly with a file or sharpening stone. Some local hardware stores will do this for you for a small fee.

## Sterilize

Sterilizing and disinfecting cutting tools such as pruning shears is important to prevent transferring disease from plant to plant. A popular method is to soak tools for a few minutes in a 1:2 bleach-to-water mix. I prefer to use hydrogen peroxide, a safer, more environmentally friendly alternative. Grapefruit seed extract also works as a disinfectant. This is a natural and potent antifungal available in concentrated liquid form from most health food stores.

## Lubricate

A classic method that both cleans and oils simultaneously is to add some oil to a bucket of sand. Return trowels and other metal tools to the oiled sand after each use to prevent rusting. Alternatively, apply a general-purpose oil with a rag or drop onto the moving or hinged parts of tools such as shears.

# NOT YOUR GRANDMOTHER'S GARDENING APRON

Gardening aprons tend to come in two styles: Suzy Homemaker or Bob the Builder. Tool belts are a practical accessory for carrying your gadgets, but that doesn't mean you have to look lame out in the garden. With beginner sewing skills you can make a handy, hardworking apron that reflects your personal style and taste. Load it up with seed packets, tags, trowels, markers, and string, and then head out to the garden with everything you need right on your waist.

## CHOOSING FABRIC

Garden aprons are a rugged accessory meant to hold heavy tools, get dirty, and take some wear and tear. A dainty kitchen apron just won't do. Select a thick, washable fabric for the outside and a lighter-weight washable fabric for the lining. Denim, cotton twill, upholstery fabric, and canvas are good thick fabric choices. Make an apron that suits your style. You can try vintage fabrics or cut up a large pair of old jeans and line it with a funky floral pillowcase.

**1.** Cut two pieces of fabric each 20 inches wide and 16 inches long. One piece will be the thicker outer fabric and the other a thinner lining.

**2.** Align your pieces, right sides facing, and secure with pins.

**3.** Sew a ½-inch seam around the edges, leaving a 5-inch opening for turning right side out. With a pair of scissors cut excess fabric from each corner, being careful not to get too close to the stitching.

**4.** Turn the piece right side out and press flat.

*You Will Need*

*½ yard each of two contrasting fabrics
*Ruler or measuring tape
*Scissors
*Pins
*Sewing machine
*Thread
*Iron
*Tailor's chalk
*1½–2 yards of 1½-inch-wide ribbon or cotton twill tape

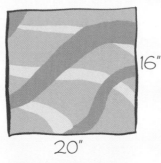

16"

20"

step 1

*Legend*

 Right side of fabric

 Lining

 Outer fabric

**5.** Sew a ¼-inch seam across the long side. This will be the top seam of your pocket later on.

**6.** Lay the full piece lining side up. Fold the bottom up, leaving a 2-inch space of lining peeking out at the top.

**7.** Sew a ¼-inch seam along each short side from the top seam all the way down to the fold. Don't forget to backstitch at the start and finish off your seams. Now you've created a rectangle with a giant pocket.

**8.** Next, divide this giant pocket into five smaller pockets, two 5 inches wide, two 3½ inches wide, and the final pocket 2 inches wide. With a ruler, measure and then mark straight lines onto the fabric with tailor's chalk.

**9.** Following the chalk lines, sew a straight line beginning at the top of the pocket down to the bottom fold.

**10.** Now that you've created the apron base, you'll need a tie to go around your waist. Your tie can be made from a piece of ribbon, cotton twill tape, bias tape, or thick, decorative trim. Fold the ribbon or tape in half width-wise and press a 20-inch crease along the center.

**11.** Center the ribbon along the top edge of the apron, fold the ribbon in half over the edge, and affix with pins. Sew a ½-inch seam along the top of the tie to secure it to the apron. For extra security, sew along the side edges.

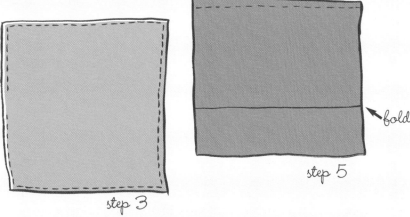

step 5

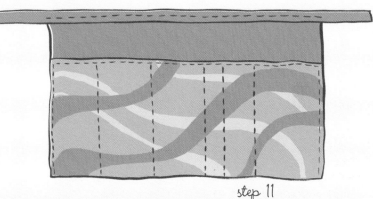

step 3

step 11

# PLANTING SEEDS

*Get Some*

Tiny seeds are abundant and easy to come by in gardening stores. But what if you want something more interesting than 'Early Girl' tomatoes and English cucumbers? A quick search online can open up a giant world of seeds with more variety than you could ever have imagined. Specialized companies sell everything from unusual heirloom plants to organic seeds and exotic jungle tree seeds. You can even buy seeds on eBay! Just be aware when buying seed from another country or state that there are laws governing the movement of plant matter across borders, including seed. Check your local or national department of agriculture or customs office for current laws and regulations. You can do that online too! (See Resources for more info.)

Most cities have ethnic neighborhoods or stores that sell seeds of crops common in other countries but unusual in North America. Vegetable and herb seeds labeled "rare" or "unusual" (and expensive) in chic urban garden stores and specialty greenhouses are often only a few bucks in Chinatown.

If you want to get your seeds free, seed exchanges and swaps are the way to go. In the early spring some cities and horticultural societies host local seed swapping events in community centers and school gyms. Canada has a national seed exchanging event called "Seedy Saturdays" where gardeners can swap with one another or purchase seeds from cottage industry and organic growers. (See Resources for a listing of North American seed trading organizations.) If you can't find a local event, try joining an online newsgroup or bulletin board. Members post their "Wanted" and "To Exchange" lists and trade through the mail. You can sign up at **YouGrowGirl.com** to be part of a round-robin group. You mail a package of seeds you don't need to another member of the group, who adds seeds and takes some, then passes it along to the next member in the group. It's a fun and almost free way to get all kinds of seeds.

## SEED-STARTING BASICS

Each small seed has the potential to become one gorgeous plant. Germination is the process of coaxing the dormant plant to come outside and play. Each seed has a will to live and will not come out if the conditions are wrong. In the early stages of germination, three things get the ball rolling: heat, soil, and water. Make it your mantra. As your seedling develops you'll need to learn a few more things, but we'll take this one step at a time.

Seeds can be started outdoors or indoors. Just about any seed can be started outside, but many fragile seedlings can benefit from cozy indoor conditions where they are watched and coddled. Some plants, including tomatoes and squash, require a long growing season and constant warmth. If you're in a cold climate, starting your seeds inside early will allow you a jump-start on the growing season.

*Seed Starting Mix*

*1 part peat or peat substitute such as coir
*1 part perlite
*1 part vermiculite

Thoroughly mix ingredients in a bucket and add water until the mix is evenly moist but not drenched.

You can also work some worm castings and/or compost into the mix. Your seedlings don't need this extra nutrition, but adding it now will save you the trouble of adding fertilizer before you transplant.

*Growing Seeds in Jell-O*

As a crazy science experiment, try growing seeds in a sterile jelly mix such as gelatin, agar-agar, or even Jell-O. This is a great way to germinate difficult plants. The gelatin will get moldy pretty quickly, so plant seedlings in a pot once they have germinated.

**Gelatin** is derived from animal bone and is high in nitrogen. Agaragar is a derivative of seaweed and is high in phosphorus, calcium, and other minerals.

Make your mix according to package directions and pour at least 2 inches into a sterilized baby food jar. Once the gel has cooled and set, lightly push your seeds into the gelatin and cover the jar with a sheet of clear plastic or glass. Place the jar in a warm spot. If mold develops, sprinkle a little powdered cinnamon on the surface. Once seeds begin to germinate, carefully remove the seedlings and place in potting mix.

## Heat

When preparing to start your seeds, pick a location that fits the first part of the mantra: heat. Most seeds will not be tempted to come out of their shell if the soil is too cool. Keep the soil temperature between 60°F and 75°F if possible. Garden centers sell special plug-in heating pads like little electric blankets that keep the soil not too hot and not too cold but just right. If you can't afford a heating pad, or just think it's silly, a warm appliance, like the top of your fridge, your VCR, or your CPU, makes a good substitute. Just be sure to use a tray to avoid damaging the hardware.

## Soil

If you've read anything else about soil in this book, you probably know that just any old soil isn't going to work. Seedlings are tender young things susceptible to all sorts of trouble. They need light, airy, sterile soil to keep them safe from fungus and disease. The soil that's out in your yard is fine in the garden but a disaster in a container. Garden soil becomes hard and compact in a pot, suffocating young seedlings and creating a breeding ground for disease. Buy seed-starting mix at the store or try making your own (see sidebar, opposite). These mixes are light and water retentive, perfect for little seedlings on the go.

Gardening stores sell cool-looking compressed peat pellets for germinating seeds. Porous peat is great for air circulation but bad for water retention. They tend to flip from super dry to super soaked, an unsteady situation for fragile seedlings. Plus they're small, which means that larger seedlings like tomatoes tend to require transplanting into a bigger container before planting outdoors. They're a pricey option, especially if you're starting a lot of seeds. Save your cash and buy a bag of starting mix. It will go a whole lot further.

## Water

Seeds need water like Homer Simpson needs donuts. Water helps crack the seed coating and quenches the thirst of a growing seedling, but too much water can rot a baby seedling before it gets a chance to sprout. Keep the soil damp, but not soaking. Think of the soil as a sponge. Your sponge should be moist when pressed but without a puddle sitting on its surface. Getting the balance right can take some practice and a few waterlogged seeds.

It'll help to water your seedling from the bottom rather than the top. Place the pot in a shallow dish and pour water into the dish. The soil sponge will soak up as much water as it needs and leave the rest. Dump excess water from the tray before an hour is up. Don't let your pot sit in a tray of water for an extended length of time.

## SUITABLE CONTAINERS

If you're sowing seeds indoors, you're going to need a container. Just about anything from store-bought cell packs to margarine containers will do the job, as long as they have holes in the bottom for drainage. Terra-cotta pots are attractive containers but not ideal for seed starting because they dry out quickly.

## SOWING

Now is when you put on your farmer gear and get started on the best part of the whole process. Moisten a batch of seed-starting mix by dumping it in a bucket and mixing in enough water to make the mix damp but not soaked. Fill each container with the premoistened seed-starting mix. Using the bottom of an identical container as a tamping device, lightly press the soil to eliminate large air bubbles. Leave a little space at the top of each container.

How you sow the seeds depends on what kind of plant it is. Your seed pack should tell you how deep to sow. Some seeds are simply sprinkled on the surface, while other seeds should be pressed into the soil and covered. A general rule of thumb is sprinkle tiny seeds and deep-sow large seeds. Sow more than one seed in a container. Two is a good number. If one seed doesn't germinate the other probably will. Place your containers in a tray, water from the bottom, and you're off and running.

Starting seeds indoors isn't always the only way to go—in fact, some plants, such as peas, poppies, beans, and nasturtiums, grow better when sown straight into the ground outdoors. This method is called **direct sowing**. How you go about it depends on the type of plant you've got. Most wildflowers can be lightly sprinkled rather haphazardly, while most veggie crops are best suited to rows, groupings, or some other sort of planned placement—not so different, really, from container-sown seeds. However, while container-sown seeds will be transplanted later, direct-sown seeds are in it for the long haul once they're in the ground. When planning the placement of seeds, try to visualize each tiny seed as a full-grown plant. This will ensure that you plant approximately the right amount of plants for your space. But don't fret—if you overplant you can always thin back a bit later.

## LABELING

Don't forget to label those seeds. I'm always sure that with all the work I've put into those seeds, I'll remember what I've sown where. I never remember. Mark cheap containers on the outside with an indelible marker, or get crafty and make your own tags. All the materials needed to create your own cool tags are on hand in the recycling bin. Old forks can be shaped into "fancy" tag holders, or vertical blinds and yogurt containers can be cut into labeling strips.

### Cheap Containers

Plastic margarine and yogurt containers, plastic bottles with the tops cut off, egg shells propped up in their carton, toilet paper rolls, plastic cups, and milk cartons are all excellent and free seed-starting containers.

### Aiding Germination

Peas, beans, and other large, hard-coated seeds can benefit from a 24-hour soak in room-temperature water before sowing. This presoak helps soften the seed coat, aiding germination.

Other hard-shelled seeds such as parsley like to be scratched against sandpaper to rough up the hard shell. This is called **scarification**.

Some seeds, especially many northern natives, require a length of time in a cool place such as a refrigerator before germination will happen. This is called **cold stratification**. The length of time required depends on the seed, so do some research before experimenting with fussy plants.

## MAKE A COPPER TAG HOLDER

**1.** Cut medium or heavy gauge copper wire to a 13-inch length.

**2.** Roll the top 8 inches into a spiral. Leave the remaining 5 inches pointing straight down as the stem. You should have a shape that resembles a fiddlehead.

**3.** Write the name of the plant on a piece of stiff paper or board. Tuck it into the spiral. Outdoor tags should be laminated or printed with indelible marker on thin plastic.

## LIGHT

Seedlings that have popped out of the soil need a lot of light—a good 12 to 16 hours per day. South-facing windows are good enough, but most windows are too dim and will produce leggy plants that grow tall and thin while trying to reach the light.

The answer is fluorescent lights. Yes, those yucky office lights that make everyone look sallow will give your seedlings all the light they need. Small incandescent grow bulbs that give off full-spectrum light are cheaper, but they get very hot and burn plants. Fluorescent lights conserve energy and won't give your plants a sunburn.

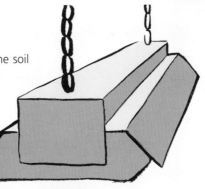

### Thrifty Light Setup

Your seedlings don't need an extravagant grow-light setup. A trip to the hardware store and twenty dollars should get you what you need. Buy an inexpensive fluorescent shop light that can be hung on a chain from the ceiling or installed beneath a shelf. Seedlings require only the cool part of the light spectrum and that's just what cool white bulbs supply. Add a self-timer so turning the system on and off is a no-brainer.

Place your plants very close to the fluorescent light and increase the distance as the plants grow. You can do this by hooking the lights up with chains or propping containers on top of other containers.

## FERTILIZING

Seedings show up with a well-packed suitcase. For the first part of their lives, they get nutrition from their cotyledon leaves. These "seed leaves" are the first things to emerge from the soil and are actually a part of the seed rather than true leaves. Seed leaves feed the baby plant until it has formed real leaves and can get down to the business of photosynthesis. You'll know it is time to fertilize your plant when the seed leaves shrivel and fall off. If you have added some worm castings (see page 95) or compost to the soil prior to planting, you won't need to fertilize until after transplanting. If not, lightly scratch a pinch of worm poo into the soil. You can also water the plants with a diluted sea-kelp mix.

## THINNING

Your little seedlings are going to shoot up like power plants. Just when they're looking their best, it's time to show some tough love. A bunch of tightly packed seedlings can become sickly as they fight for root space, light, and nutrition. It's a brutal job, but sacrificing a few will be worth it in the long run. You should not have more than two seedlings growing in a pot. In the case of seeds grown in rows, refer to your original seed packet for information on how close is too close.

To thin, snip off stems at the soil level using a sharp pair of scissors. The snipped plant will wither and die. Trying to remove the seedling root and all seems like a good idea, but it will only disturb and damage the delicate root systems of surrounding plants.

## HARDENING OFF

The gardening season is kicking off, your seedlings have developed five true leaves, and it's time to get them outside. This is your plant's make-it-or-break-it moment. Inside, your seedlings had it easy in a cushy environment, but outside they'll have to rough it in the real world of high winds, pounding rain, hot sun, and cool nights. Plopping them outside and hoping they'll fend for themselves is a risky proposition. Instead, give them a chance to adjust to the great big world through a slow transition called "hardening off."

Most seedlings will not survive even short periods of frost, so be sure to research the forecast in your area before beginning the hardening-off process. Alternatively, check out *The Farmer's Almanac*, the planting bible, or go online at www.almanac.com.

Bring your tray of seedlings outside and set it in a sheltered, shady location. If you don't have a shady spot, make a newspaper triangle and prop it over the tray of plants. Bring everything back inside after an hour or two. Over the course of two weeks, slowly increase the length of time the plants spend outside while also gradually introducing them to sunnier locations. Halt the process on particularly cold days. By the end of the second week, your plants should be staying outside overnight and be ready to plant in the garden.

At this stage, rodents can be a risk in urban and some suburban locations. Squirrels, raccoons, and rats can't resist tender seedlings and fresh dirt. If you fear four-legged fiends, cover your seedlings with a layer of light plastic. If you have a car, you can use it as a mobile hardening-off station. Just be sure to protect the plants from the harsh, magnified sun that comes through glass windows. Leave the windows cracked slightly to allow air circulation.

# PROTECTING YOUR BABIES

The sooner you get edible plants outside the sooner you can begin harvesting the goods. A cloche or bell jar is a Victorian-style and rather cool-looking greenhouse contraption used to protect seedlings from harsh wind, torrential rains, and chilly weather. They provide warmth and humidity around tender plants during their formative first days. Your baby plant will be as snug as the boy in the bubble and protected against squirrels and raccoons, slugs and insects.

The real thing can fetch a high price at antique stores these days, but you can make your own from materials lying around the house.

**1.** Remove the cap and labels from your bottle.

**2.** Cut an inch off the bottom of the bottle using a serrated knife. You've made a cloche!

**3.** Place the cloche over your seedling and bury it an inch or two into the soil for support.

**4.** Remove the cloche when the plant outgrows it, or cut off the top half and leave it around the plant as a protective ring against slugs and cutworms.

### You Will Need

*Plastic bottle or jug (any size)
*Serrated knife

### Tip

Glass mason jars also make attractive bell jars. Scour thrift stores and garage sale for jars made of green glass or adorned with cool, old-school typography. Don't let your plants suffocate—prop the jar up now and again to provide some air circulation.

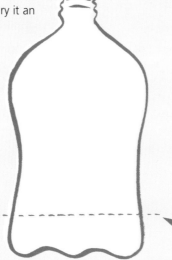

*cut here*

# ONE, TWO, THREE, PLANT

Now that your grown-up plants or seedlings are ready to go into the ground or into a pot, what do you do? Follow these basic steps for getting your seedling or nursery plants growing in your garden.

## GROUND PLANTING

**1.** Dig a hole. Your hole should be twice the width of the root mass of the plant. It should be deep enough so that the crown of the plant (where the root meets the stem) is level with the soil surface—you don't want the crown to rot underground. Some plants such as tomatoes are an exception and should be planted more deeply so their stems can produce extra roots.

**2.** Sprinkle some dry fertilizer such as sea kelp, compost, or worm castings into the hole if you choose.

**3.** Gently remove your plant from its current pot. Squeezing the sides of plastic pots will release the plant. Terra-cotta or other hard pots may need to be tilted over and tapped from the bottom. If the pot has a large enough drainage hole, push your finger through to ease the root ball from the pot.

**4.** Place the plant in the hole and backfill with soil around the roots. Press the soil firmly.

**5.** Lay some mulch on top if you choose. Mulch should not be laid over the crown. You can also sprinkle some dry fertilizer on the surface if you wish.

**6.** Water your plant in liberally. For larger plants, dig a shallow moat around the perimeter of the plant. This will hold the water around the roots, preventing runoff.

*dig a hole*

*squeeze the sides of the pot*

*backfill the hole with soil and press firmly*

## CONTAINER PLANTING

**1.** If your pot has a large drainage hole, place a shard of broken pot or piece of cut screening in the bottom to prevent soil from escaping out the bottom.

**2.** If your container is not much larger than your plant, fill it one-half to three-quarters full with soil. Push some of that soil off to the sides to form a deeper hole in the middle. If you're planting in a large pot, fill it entirely with soil, then dig a hole in the center that is large enough to accommodate the plant's root-ball.

**3.** Gently remove your plant from its pot. See item 3 under Ground Planting for details.

**4.** Sometimes a container-grown plant becomes root-bound in the pot. Once it's out of the pot, you may discover your plant's roots are compacted into a tight mass. It's not a problem—just gently pry the roots apart with your fingertips.

step 6

**5.** Place the plant in the hole in its new home. The crown of the plant (where the root meets the stem) should be level with the soil surface. Some plants such as tomatoes are an exception, as their stems will actually produce roots if buried. Most other plants will rot if their crown is buried.

**6.** Press the surrounding soil around the root-ball. Add more soil if required to completely surround the root mass. There should be an inch or so of space between the soil and the top of the pot.

**7.** Add a layer of mulch if you'd like.

**8.** Water the plant well.

pot-bound root ball

### They're Growing Up

Inevitably your plant will become pot-bound—grow too big for its pot. All plants grow at their own rate, so there is no fixed time to repot. You'll know it's time to bust out some new digs when roots start snaking their way out the drainage holes. For repotting, follow the same method as for container planting. Severely pot-bound plants—those with a root-ball that has become very tight and entwined—may need some extra work. Gently tease the roots a bit to give them a head start at spreading out before placing in a larger container. If the roots are extremely tight, you can resort to slicing the solid mass in half or thirds from the bottom up with a sharp, clean knife. Make cuts that run about a third up the length of the root-ball.

# COMPANION PLANTING

Companion planting is the chance to create a love fest in your garden. By grouping plants that cooperate instead of compete, you get the plants to do the hard work and thrive. A familiar example of companion planting is the combo of marigolds and tomatoes—the marigolds repel pests that love tomatoes. Different combinations of plants can solve many of your potential garden woes. Some plants are good for the nutrition of the soil while others will attract beneficial insects to the garden. Companion planting can be enlisted as wind protection and to provide shade. The benefits are endless!

## COMPANION PLANTING CHART

### Soil and Plant Boosters

These plants act as health tonics and helpmates in the garden, improving soil nutrition or aiding the immune systems of their companions.

* Plant white valerian with sick plants.
* Plant shallow-rooted plants such as lettuce with taprooted plants like carrot. The taproot pulls nutrients up to the surface.
* Plant clover, which fixes nitrogen, near cabbage and broccoli.

### Pest Resistance

Grow these plants or combinations to give your garden a running head start against insect pests.

* Marigolds prevent nematodes (microscopic worms).
* Potatoes and beans together confuse the Mexican bean beetle and the Colorado potato beetle. Or try corn, squash, and beans in a traditional grouping called the Three Sisters.
* Garlic and roses.
* Rue and roses.
* Coriander and potatoes.
* Interplanting carrots and onions will confuse pests.

### Flavor Enhancers

Herbs are a taste sensation in the garden as well as the cooking pot. Growing specific herbs in combination with other edibles is said to promote the flavor of their companions. Try these pairs:

* Basil and tomatoes
* Bee balm and tomatoes
* Borage and strawberry
* Borage and tomatoes
* Chervil with radishes
* German chamomile with onions
* Yarrow and herbs

# CHALKBOARD POTS

Every time I plant a fabulous new farmer's market find or a contraband clipping, I'm sure I'll remember this unique plant's name. A week later I stare at the pot wondering what the heck this leafy stick really is.

A crafty solution is to use chalkboard paint to fashion plain ol' terra-cotta pots into containers cooler than the ones found at the local garden center—and have the label built right in!

Pre-designed label templates are available on page 202, or flex your crafting muscles and design your own.

**1.** Photocopy or scan and print out one of the label designs. Lay the design flat on the cutting mat and place a piece of Mylar on top. Tape down both the design and the Mylar to secure.

**2.** Cut along the lines of the design with a sharp X-Acto knife. This is your stencil.

**3.** Determine placement of the design on your pot and affix with tape. Be certain that the inside of the stencil shape is lying flat against the pot to avoid messing up the edges of the design with smeared paint.

## You Will Need

* Preprinted label design (found on page 202) or your own label design
* A cutting mat
* Mylar
* X-Acto knife
* Tape
* Clean terra-cotta pots (with or without rims)
* Newspaper
* Sponge brush
* Can of chalkboard paint (your choice of color)
* Chalk

**4.** Protect your work surface with a layer of newspaper. Using the sponge brush, carefully apply a coat of paint to the exposed part of your stencil. Set aside to dry.

**5.** When the first coat is thoroughly dry, apply a second coat. If you like an aged look, skip this step and paint the first coat thinly.

**6.** Let the paint cure for several days before planting up the pots.

**7.** Rub the chalkboard surface of the pots with the long edge of a piece of white chalk. Rub it off. Now your chalking surface is prepped for use.

**8.** Use any colored chalk to write the name of the plant on the chalk paint.

### More Ideas

❊ For a simple pot, paint the entire surface with chalk paint or apply paint to the rim only.

❊ Little pots can be used for starting seeds, and you won't forget what's in them.

# GROW

Some gardeners go wild designing their space and love to spend their garden-time building trellises, constructing paths, and shopping for garden gnomes at local flea markets. Others get their garden on by lavishing attention on their plants. For every gardener the business of making baby plants and getting them into the ground is monumental. But keeping your little plants alive and healthy and your garden flourishing is the real challenge—and half the fun!

When there's trouble in paradise, as there often is, your first instinct may be to reach for the spray bottle to perform a quick fix. The information contained in the Grow chapter will lead you through the basics of keeping plants healthy over the long term, providing wash-and-wear care instructions, troubleshooting tips, and easy preventative medicine while guiding you through the fundamentals of your plants' needs and how to meet them. And if trouble does find its way into your garden, I offer natural and low-budget alternatives to keep the peace in your green domain.

This chapter also dishes the dirt on one of the most rewarding gardening activities: growing organic food. Homegrown is the way to go for super-delicious tomatoes and a never-ending supply of scrumptuous salad greens! In this chapter you'll learn how easy it is to grow the best veggies you've ever tasted, gorgeous and totally edible ornamentals, and beginner crops especially suited to containers and small spaces. You can grow enough on your first try to embellish your home-made meals, or possibly enough to stockpile some tasty morsels for winter.

# GROWING ORGANIC

Buying organic veggies and chicken is about as trendy as miniskirts right now. Everybody's getting into it, or at least wishing they could. There's a very good reason behind all this hoopla. We all know organic is better for the environment, better for the world's soil, and better for our health. And organic food tastes a whole lot better! But what does the big O (Organic!) mean for your garden?

If you're laying off the chemicals and synthetic fertilizers, you are already halfway there. Organic gardening means gardening naturally without the use of chemicals, but it is also about building a healthy garden that relies on a supportive interaction between your plants and the soil they are growing in. Most organic gardeners consider their number-one job growing the soil as a living organism. Job number two is actually growing plants.

Many new or aspiring gardeners assume that growing organic is difficult or confusing. However, with a little knowledge and experience you will discover that growing organically can actually save work by preventing problems before they start. It also means that when that first warm, sun-ripened tomato appears on the vine, you can pluck it off and pop it into your mouth without the concern of eating a pile of nasty chemicals. Heaven!

# GOOD GROWING BASICS

The first step in creating a garden is getting to know your space and climate and what it can or can't provide. Beginners should opt out of growing a lush, tropical oasis in the Midwest or a desert landscape in the Northeast. Once you've got that down, it's time to get to get familiar with some plants and their needs (especially if you've bought them already!). All plants need varying degrees of three basic requirements to grow and thrive: light, water, and nutrition. It's best if you can find out how much of each your plant will require before making a commitment to it. Once you have the plant, experiment until you've reached a happy balance. If you can, find out about the natural habitat of your plant. Check out the details online or in a book, or go to your plant's natural habitat if you can and observe it in the wild. Understanding the natural living conditions of a plant will go a long way toward understanding how to make it happy.

## LIGHT

Everyone covets a bright, sunny garden bursting with colorful blooms and luscious vegetables. However, it's not all sunshine and roses for the hot tar rooftop or heat-conducting metal fire escape—the full-sun icon on the plant tag doesn't include the fiery depths of hell! Never fear, some plants will thrive in the super full-sun environment, but getting to know which ones have what it takes requires some enthusiastic experimentation. Look for Mediterranean or desert plants such as cacti and succulents or plants that are labeled "drought tolerant" or "heat tolerant." Generally plants with silver foliage, succulent leaves, or small leaves can take extra heat and sun. If you can, alter your environment to provide some shade. Large trees or vines can be grown to shade smaller plants. Bolt a gazebo down to a wood deck or build permanent protection from wood and corrugated plastic sheeting. A piece of cheap lace draped over sensitive plants on the hottest days is a budget- and fashion-conscious option. The key to survival in really hot conditions is getting a good, long drink of water regularly.

You can always put a damper on intense heat, but you can't do anything to manufacture brighter light and more sun. If your space is quite shady or receives only a few hours of sun per day, then you may have to resign yourself to shade-tolerant plants. Believe me, it's not the end of the world! There are lots of gorgeous and exciting shade-lovers to choose from. While plant tags will tell you what's what at the store, you can also tell by the leaf shape: most shade-dwelling plants have large, wide leaves, to gather the most light possible.

## WATER AND HUMIDITY

Plants need water to survive. Not enough water and your plant shrivels up and dies. But too much of a good thing is a common problem in gardening. Along with causing root rot, overwatering trains your plants to be lazy and weak, making their roots grow shallow along the surface rather than digging down and creating some stability.

It depends on the weather and your garden's conditions, but it's a good idea to water your plants well when they are first getting established after planting and then cut back a bit once they take off. Water in-ground plants only once a week if the weather isn't too hot and intense.

Container-grown plants are a whole different ball game. They dry out much faster than in-ground plants. Plants growing on hot rooftops may require as much as one or two waterings daily during the hottest days of summer. How much water depends on the number of plants per container and the plant size. Large plants or tightly packed containers dry out fast.

Don't let your containers dry out completely! Bone dry soil, especially if it's a peat-based mix, will become hydrophobic, meaning it will repel water rather than absorbing it. Water rushes quickly down the sides of the container and out through the bottom while plants that you think you're watering are actually drying up.

### When to Water

Try not to put off watering until too late in the evening. Cool, moist foliage attracts slugs to an evening banquet and encourages fungal diseases. During heat spells and in the middle of sunny afternoons aren't great times either, because water droplets lie on leaves like tiny magnifying lenses, charring sensitive foliage. The early morning is ideal, but since we're not all early birds, try to hit it at a cool time of day, allowing enough time for water to evaporate off the leaves before nightfall. Most importantly, water directly on the soil rather than wildly spraying all over the place with the hose or watering can. Wet leaves hold humidity, making them susceptible to fungal disease like powdery mildew.

# SIMPLE IRRIGATION SYSTEM

On hot summer days, this cheap and easy drip system provides a constant stream of water to your plants. You can make it from materials in your recycling bin, and it's top-notch for tomatoes and other plants that require deep watering and loathe wet leaves. Add fertilizer to the mix and get it directly where your plant likes it best, at the roots.

**1.** Drill 4 to 8 small holes in the cap of a plastic bottle. For slower flow, make fewer holes rather than smaller holes. Tiny holes will quickly become blocked by soil and debris.

**2.** Cut off the bottom of the bottle with a serrated knife to create a funnel. Screw the cap back on.

**3.** Dig a hole next to your plant or between a group of plants that is deep enough to bury at least one-third of the bottle. Set the bottle into the hole cap-side down and press dirt around to hold it in place. Fill the bottle with water or liquid fertilizer.

The water will slowly seep into the soil, giving your plants an extended drink. Don't forget to refill the bottles when they're running low!

cut here

## You Will Need

*Empty plastic water or soda bottles (any size, with caps)
*Drill and ¼-inch bit
*Serrated knife

## Dealing with Drought

Small-space gardeners in all kinds of climates often experience droughtlike conditions. Hot decks and fire escapes are notoriously dry, parched landscapes. Before designing your garden, try to imagine what it's going to be like on the hottest, driest days of summer. Now look around your space. Do you have an outdoor tap? If not, how will you get water from the nearest source to your plants? How many plants do you plan to grow? How big will they get? How much water will they consume?

Get the picture? Follow these tips to help deal with drought.

✳ **Xeriscape**—Xeriscaping uses drought-resistant or drought-tolerant plants. Thirsty plants require heavy doses of water, but drought-tolerant plants can take short dry spells. The best plants are native to your location and climate. These plants are hardy and well adapted to your local conditions.

✳ **Mulch**—Never leave your soil bare and exposed. Even containers can be mulched with pebbles or straw. Mulch holds water in and keeps soil cool.

✳ **Catch Water**—Place empty buckets outside during heavy rains. That's one less bucket you'll have to carry outside tomorrow! If you have a roof gutter, you can take it one step further and set up a real rain barrel. You can catch water on a smaller scale by placing trays under your plant containers. The plants will suck the water in through wicking action. Keep in mind that some plants don't like wet feet. For those plants, dump excess water after an hour or so.

✳ **Get a Coil Hose**—Coil hoses are perfect for small apartments with no outdoor tap. They are compact and small enough to fit through open windows. I hook mine up to the bathroom tap and dangle it out the window. It doesn't take up much space, but it's long enough to make it out to the farthest reaches of my deck.

✳ **Let It Drip**—Make a drip irrigation system from a plastic bottle (see opposite page). Drip systems release water slowly as it is needed.

## Water Conservation and Recycling

Water your plants with old aquarium water, gray water (used dish-, bath-, or laundry water); water used to boil eggs, pasta, or veggies; leftover tea and coffee (only for acid-loving plants). Put a bucket under the tap while you're waiting for the water to get hot in your third-floor apartment. Rig up a rain barrel that collects water from the gutters or collect water in buckets during a heavy rainfall.

# SUCCULENT CONTAINER

Succulents are super troopers that often thrive in sunny, dry regions of the garden. Exposed decks, rooftops, and fire escapes are particularly tough locations to garden and require plants that can take a fair amount of hardship. When all else fails, send in the succulents!

Succulents are known as warm-climate plants, but you'd be surprised by the selection that will survive through cold winters. Check the growing conditions to be sure yours is suited to life outdoors in your climate. If not, just pack it up and bring it in before the first frost and provide it with a nice, sunny location indoors until next summer.

## GROWING

### Soil

All succulents must be provided with good drainage or they will rot. Use containers that have at least one drainage hole, and add holes if necessary. Plant in a well-draining mix similar to the one shown in the box at right. A layer of rocks or a cool-looking mulch on the soil surface will keep the sandy mix from sloshing out when watered and keep your succulents looking stylie. Try grit, aquarium gravel, marbles, or pebbles.

### Water

Succulents prefer to dry out for a short period between watering.

### Light

Full sun, super sun.

### Fertilizing

Succulents don't eat much. Dilute balanced houseplant mixes by half and fertilize sparingly at the start of the growing season only.

### Succulent Mix

* 1 part pumice
* 2 parts sand
* 3 parts compost

# THE PLANTS

## Cold Climate (Hardy)

**Hens and chicks (*Sempervivum* species)**—Known as house leek in the U.K., sempervivums are a mainstay of the 1950s mod rock garden. Everyone and their uncle has grown them at one time or another, ruining the reputation of this remarkable plant. Hens and chicks are at their best when clumped together to form a mesmerizing array of rosettes. In midsummer, a blooming cluster resembles alien starships reaching for the mother ship. Those of the Gothic persuasion will appreciate *Sempervivum arachnoideum*, a peculiar variety that appears to be draped in a blanket of cobwebbing.

**Stonecrop (*Sedum* species)**—Stonecrop come in a vast array of shapes, colors and sizes. Propagation is often as easy as chucking a leaf in some soil. They are frequently trailing plants, perfect for hanging baskets and window boxes. Sedums and sempervivums make great companions in shallow dish gardens. Pair the red foliage of *Sedum spurium* 'Dragon's Blood' with a clump of cobweb sempervivum. A personal favorite is *Sedum spathulifolium* 'Cape Blanco', a dusty silver variety with tiny spiral rosettes.

## Warm Climate (Tender)

**Echeveria**—Echeveria resemble oversized, silvery blue hens and chicks. Like hens and chicks they are best grouped together or grown individually in a small container. Watch out—they will not survive cold winters outdoors.

**Agave**—You'll likely know agave as the tequila plant, but to ancient Mesoamericans it was the near center of a culture. Modernists love it for its fierce architectural form and minimal care requirements. Long spines make it a bit of a hazard, so keep it somewhere sunny but out of the way. Species such as *Agave parryi* and *Agave havardiana* do well in cooler climates.

## TIP

Hardy plants can survive a deep freeze in the garden. Tender plants cannot survive a winter freeze and must be brought indoors in northern climates.

## PLANTS TO TRY

### Cold Climate (Hardy):

* Hedgehog cactus (*Echinocereus* species)
* Spurge (*Euphorbia myrsinites*)
* Winter hardy prickly pear (*Opuntia humifusa*)
* Yucca

### Warm Climate (Tender):

* Aeonium (*Aeonium arboreum*)
* Aloe
* Mother-in-law's tongue (*Sansevieria trifasciata*)

# FERTILIZING

Want to strike fear in the heart of a new gardener? Just mention fertilizing. Scary!

Most new gardeners understand that plants need nutrients. But what do you feed a plant? And how? Once you're at the garden store, it doesn't get any better. Liquid fish meal or a bag of chemicals seem to be the only options.

The intimidation factor is probably the most common reason why gardeners reach for the powdered, synthetic fertilizers—all you have to do is mix it up, pour it on, and watch your plant do a Jack and the Beanstalk.

If synthetic fertilizers are so easy, why not stick with them? It comes down to this: chemical fertilizers are a quick fix. They give individual plants a temporary boost. But natural, organic fertilizers build a healthy, self-sustaining environment for your plant. They help you grow an entire system, not just an individual plant.

What do you do if you're trying to go au naturel? It turns out that fertilizing basically means replacing the depleted nitrogen, phosphorus, and potassium in your plants' soil. Instead of mixing up a bag of synthetic chemicals, you can add natural sources of these minerals to your soil to make it healthy and chemical-free.

## Synthetic versus Organic

* Synthetics harm the soil, destroying helpful microorganisms.
* Synthetics are high in salts (shows as crystaline buildup on the surface of pots), which make your plants thirsty.
* Synthetics give a sudden burst of nutrients and can burn plants on contact. Some brands must not be sprayed directly on foliage.
* Organics build the soil, making a healthy, self-sustaining system.
* Organics increase organic content and water-holding capacity of soil.
* Organics release nutrients slowly without burning sensitive plant parts. Some can even be sprayed directly on foliage.

## What Are Those Numbers?

A bottle or bag of fertilizer, whether synthetic or organic, usually displays a set of three numbers that look something like this: 6-6-4. These three numbers are called the NPK ratio and refer to the relative proportions of three main nutrients in fertilizers: nitrogen, phosphorus, and potassium (in that order). Plants require a host of trace minerals and secondary nutrients beyond these, but these are the three biggies. This numbers business can seem like an added chore; however, understanding the numbers on the bag will help you choose the right fertilizer mix for the job. As an example, leafy plants prefer nitrogen-rich fertilizers for growing lush and green, so choose a mix that shows the first number listed (nitrogen) as the highest. A balanced fertilizer has an equal proportion of all three nutrients and can be used as a general all-purpose fertilizer. No sweat.

## How to Fertilize

Fertilizers can be worked into the soil at the beginning or end of each growing season. Most plants, especially flowers and veggies, will require small amounts added once every two weeks during the growing season. Pay close attention to your plants. See "Become a Plant Whisperer" on page 92 for more on spotting nutrient deficiency.

Don't overdose! Getting heavy-handed with fertilizer is the easiest and fastest way to kill a plant. Underfertilized plants actually grow better than overfertilized plants. When in doubt, don't!

For more information see "Nutrients and Deficiencies" on page 45.

## Fertilizing Tips

* Fertilize during the growing season only. Give your plants a break during the winter or whenever they've gone dormant.
* Give your plants a good drink of water after applying fertilizer.
* The best time to apply fertilizer is in the morning before the hot sun is out.

# ORGANIC FERTILIZERS

*(Arranged from highest to lowest nutritional content)*

## Balanced Organic Matter (Equal NPK)

* **Worm Castings**—Worm poo has got to be one of the greatest miracles of the natural world. It is odorless, dry, can be stored for long periods of time, and is a good source of rich, earthy humus. Mix it into seed-starting mix or add a sprinkle before transplanting. It's also good for general fertilizing at any time. Making your own is easy and will provide you with lots and lots of it for free! (See Subterranean Worm World, page 95.)

* **Compost**—You can't go wrong with compost. It's a great soil additive and rich in all kinds of good stuff. What goes into compost is what comes out, so the nutritional content varies from batch to batch depending on what the compost was made from.

## Nitrogen

Nitrogen affects leaf growth. Nitrogen-rich soil produces lush, healthy foliage. But watch out! Too much nitrogen causes lush foliage and poor, pathetic flower and fruit production. It's easy to overdose on nitrogen, so if you see the signs that there is too much, cut out applications and wait until it leaches from the soil.

* **Bloodmeal**—Bloodmeal is just as gory as it sounds: blood that has been collected from the slaughterhouse and dried. It is very high in nitrogen, but can be a little overbearing as a result. Too much will burn plants or lead to a nitrogen overdose. On application, bloodmeal reeks of death and decay but does make a good rodent and pest deterrent. Add bloodmeal sparingly early in the growing season by scratching a little into the soil surface around plants.

* **Fish Emulsion**—A by-product of the fishing industry, fish emulsion is a high-nitrogen supplement made from mashed-up fish scraps. It isn't as nitrogen concentrated as bloodmeal and contains a wide breadth of trace minerals. It stinks of rotten fish and may attract a few unwanted mammals to the garden in the first day. By the second day the smell subsides and your plants are happy.

* **Coffee Grounds**—Surprisingly, your leftover coffee grounds are loaded with nitrogen. But, not surprisingly, they're also too acidic for most plants. You can mix in something alkaline like crushed oyster shells (purchased from a farm supply store or garden center) to lower acidity before giving your plants a caffeinated nitrogen boost.

* **Manure**—The nitrogen content depends on how fresh the manure is and what kind of poo you're dealing with. All manure is not created equal. The nutritional content depends on factors such as the type of animal it came from and the animal's diet. Manure can come from cows, pigs, chickens, and even bats (called guano). Pet waste, on the other hand, is a potential health hazard to you, your pets, and your plants. Do not use manure collected from your cat's litter box or daily walks with Rover. Fresh manure must be aged before it's added to the soil or you'll burn your plants. Just because the source is organic and not synthetic does not mean the animals were raised organically. Check the label for a certified organic stamp, or ask.

## Phosphorus (Phosphate)

Phosphorus is a general health food for plants. It's essential for flowering, developing healthy fruit, and resisting disease. Seedlings need phosphorus to develop healthy, strong root systems. Dig a little into the soil when transplanting seedlings into your garden to give them an all-around boost.

* **Bonemeal**—Bonemeal is essentially, you guessed it, ground-up bones. It's a good slow-but-steady fertilizer that will last about a year. Some gardeners don't like it because it comes from animals that may not have been raised organically. Add a little to the soil alongside your plants (called side dressing) or work into the soil every spring.

* **Rock Phosphate**—Rock phosphate is mined from rocky deposits of prehistoric animals. It's a great source of phosphorus, but if your soil is too alkaline it won't get absorbed. If that seems complicated, opt for bonemeal instead. Rock phosphate is one of those amenders that should be added in the spring or fall as a side dressing or worked into the soil with a hoe. It releases nutrients quite slowly, so you really need to do this only once every few years.

## Potassium (Potash)

Potassium is the plant stress reliever, helping cranky plants cope with brief periods of cold, heat, and drought. It is responsible for producing sturdy stems and regulating the flow of nutrients through the plant system.

* **Kelp Meal**—Kelp meal is chock-full of potassium and also contains lots of trace elements. It's a great soil conditioner and can be used frequently. Fertilizer freshly brewed from dried kelp leaves a stink, but bottled liquid concentrate does all the work with less odor and labor. It can be a bit of a challenge brewing up batches of hot, stinky kelp. Price is the trade-off between the two types. A bag of dried kelp is cheap and will see you through several gardening seasons, while a bottle of liquid concentrate carries a heartier price tag and lasts about a year. Use kelp meal for foliar feeding and a quick potassium boost (see "Foliar Feeding," page 94).

* **Greensand**—Greensand is mined from marine mineral deposits and contains many trace minerals as well as potassium. This is a really slow-release fertilizer, so dig some into potassium-deficient soil once and leave it.

## BECOME A PLANT WHISPERER

If you look closely, your plants will tell you where the soil is lacking nutritionally. Get familiar with the look of your plants when they are healthy, so you'll know when something just ain't right. Use this chart to identify when it's time to add a specific nutrient.

* **Phosphorus**—Phosphorus-deficient plants have what seem like healthy, dark green leaves except that they are often small and slow growing. Phosphorus-deficient tomato seedlings typically have dark green leaves with purple undersides.

* **Nitrogen**—Plants that lack nitrogen have stunted, yellow, and/or pale leaves while the stems are thin and weak. Vegetable plants produce only a few sad, miserable-looking fruits.

* **Potassium**—When your plants need potassium they produce healthy-looking new leaves, but older foliage will often twist and curl, turning from yellow to brown along the edges before dropping off completely. Plants produce few flowers or fruit, all of which are sickly and of poor quality.
* **Calcium**—A sure sign of calcium deficiency is the presence of a tomato disease called blossom-end rot. Plants produce fruit with a yucky brown, wet-looking spot on their underside.
* **Magnesium**—When magnesium is missing older leaves turn yellow while the veins stay green.
* **Iron**—Young foliage appears white or light yellow between the veins while older leaves remain green when the plant isn't getting enough iron.

## RANK TEA

Plants like a drink now and then of a stinky, nutrient-rich tea infused from manure or compost. Teas can be poured onto the soil or sprayed directly onto leaves. While it may seem like a big, disgusting hassle to make the tea, it is totally worth the effort.

A tea made from matured compost and applied directly to the foliage gives ailing plants, especially those under attack by a fungal disease, a power boost where they need it most. Compost takes time to break down in the soil, while compost tea makes extra nutrients and good microbes available to the plant fast and furious (but in a good way).

## TO MAKE TEA

### You Will Need

*1 old stocking
*1 part compost or aged manure
*Large bucket
*5 parts water
*Molasses (optional)

**1.** Pack the compost or manure into the leg of an old stocking—like tea into a tea bag. This will save work straining later on. Tie off the top of the stocking and drop it into the bucket. Add 5 parts water.

**2.** Set the bucket aside to age for as long as 2 or 3 weeks. Some people swear by a small helping of molasses to get the microbial action going. Stir your mixture every day if you can. Keep it covered. The mix should bubble, foam, and generally stink like something nasty! When the foaming and bubbling action has subsided, you're left with a bucket of concentrated liquid goodness.

**3.** Dilute the mix to 1 part concentrate and 10 parts water before use. Pour into a spray bottle and spritz directly onto plants or pour onto soil. Fertilizer teas stink, so use them up fast!

## FOLIAR FEEDING

Some chemical fertilizers burn sensitive plant foliage, but natural fertilizers can be sprayed directly on leaves to give plants a peppy zing. Spray your plants every two weeks with a tea made from sea kelp, compost, manure, or herbs to keep them healthy and disease-free. Spray sick plants with tea made from herbs such as comfrey, stinging nettle, or horsetail. Comfrey contains magnesium, potassium, and phosphorus, while nettles are high in iron, sulphur, and magnesium. Horsetail is rich in silica, which builds strong plant tissue. It's a great way to use up invasive herbs that are taking over your garden. Compost and manure teas can be made following the directions shown for Rank Tea on the previous page.

### To Make Plant-Pepping Herbal Tea

**1.** Mix 1 part fresh herbs (include leaves, flowers, and stems) and 2 parts water in a plastic bucket.

**2.** Allow to steep for 24 hours. Place the bucket in the sun for a stronger infusion.

**3.** Strain out the herbs and pour the mix into a spray bottle.

If you can pull it off, spray your plants every 2 weeks during the growing season. The spray can be kept indefinitely, but since it will become gross over time, it's best to use it up sooner rather than later.

# SUBTERRANEAN WORM WORLD

You can easily turn out grade-A, stink-free, all-natural fertilizer for your garden, even under the kitchen sink. It's easy to build a vermicomposter (worms do the work) that can be set up in a tiny bachelorette apartment. You'll be producing stink-free gardening gold in no time.

**1.** You can buy a prefabricated, super-special worm bin from environmental stores and some garden shops, but since these are really just plastic bins with holes, spare the expense and make your own. Get a nice medium to large plastic bin with a lid. The bin should be approximately 18 inches wide. Depth is less important than width. I suggest a 15-inch-deep container.

**2.** Drill five holes in the lid, one in each corner and the fifth in the center.

**3.** Drill twelve holes in the bottom of the box. Follow the configuration shown in diagram 2.

**4.** Rip up newspaper into thin strips. You don't need to get fancy with it, just tear as thinly as you can until you've got enough strips to fill half the bin loosely. If you've got an electric paper shredder, use that for easy-peasy shredding.

**5.** Place the paper strips in the bin and fluff them up a bit. Spray the paper strips with water until they are moist, but not soaking. Too much water will drown your poor worms. The goal here is to make a soft, moist environment for them. They're going to eat the paper!

**6.** Now it's time to introduce your worms to their new spread. Place them into one corner of the bin and cover them over with paper. Worms don't like the light.

**7.** Place the bin in a cool, dark location that does not experience any major temperature fluctuations. Red wigglers can withstand some change but will not survive extremes such as freezing or frying. Keep your bin in a spot that is protected from bright light. Under the sink is perfect and convenient as is the garage (must not freeze) or the basement.

## You Will Need

* Large plastic bin or prefab worm bin
* Drill and a ¼-inch bit
* One newspaper
* Spray bottle of water
* 1 pound of red worms, aka "red wigglers" (*Eisenia foetida*)

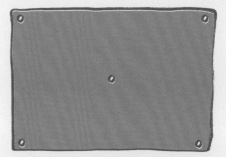

*the lid*

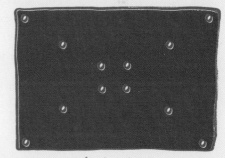

*the bin bottom*

**8.** After a day in their new home, your worms will be ready to gorge themselves. Don't just throw an entire apple into the bin. Red wigglers are voracious eaters, but they prefer their dinner chopped up and refined. Loosely chop up bits of veggie scraps and peels into 1-inch pieces. For a bin this size, place a cup or so of worm food in the top left corner of the bin and bury it under a few inches of paper. Do not spread the contents all over the bin. Burying the food keeps down bad smells and prevents fruit flies and other bugs from getting in on the action. Remember, red wigglers don't like the light; if you leave the food on top it may not get eaten up.

**9.** Two days to a week later, add another cup or so of waste to the next corner and bury it. Repeat every 2 to 7 days until you have added food to each corner. Wait a few more days and return to the first corner. By this time the waste should be gone and you can start all over with the same cycle.

## WHERE TO FIND WORMS

Getting the worms is the tricky part. Do not go out into the garden and dig up a bunch of regular old earthworms, dew worms, or night crawlers; they will not survive life in a bin. Vermicomposting is the specialty of a worm called the red wriggler that lives in compost and poo where the temperature is warm and snuggly. Red wrigglers go by many names, including red worm, poo worm, compost worm, manure worm, and fish worm. To be certain you've got the real deal, ask for it by the scientific name, *Eisenia foetida*.

You'll need to track down a supplier in your town who breeds this type of worm. Environmental stores, garden centers, and bait shops (for fishing) can hook you up. Red wrigglers are happy little breeders, so you may be able to get some free from a friend or neighbor with a population explosion. If you can't find them locally, locate a retailer online who will deliver to your neck of the woods.

## MAINTAINING YOUR BIN

Red wrigglers need a moist environment to stay happy and healthy. If the bin gets too dry or too wet you may find worms making a mad dash for drainage holes or the nearest exit the next time you lift the lid. If the bin is too wet, lift the lid slightly to air it out. If the bedding is too dry, give it a spritz or two of water.

### Food for the Worm Bin

* Fruit and veggie peels
* Rotten veggies and fruit
* Crushed eggshells
* Coffee grounds (sparingly)
* Tea leaves

### Bad for the Bin

* Anything cooked in oil
* Meat
* Bones
* Plastic and other inorganic waste
* Litter box waste

### Wormy Liquid

Place a tray underneath worm bins to catch any liquid runoff. Save the drippings and use it as a nutritional foliar spray on lanky indoor plants.

# HARVEST TIME

Within a few months you should find the bedding inside the bin turning into a black, pellet-like soil. You'll need to separate these worm castings (aka worm poo) from the worms themselves. Thankfully you will not need to do this one worm at a time. Instead, push all the bedding to one side of the container. Shred up lots of new, fresh paper and moisten it like you did when you first set your bin up. Start placing fresh food on the new side of the bin only.

After a few weeks the worms will happily migrate over to the new side where food is abundant. All you'll have to do is scoop out the castings from the old corner and divide the goodness among your plants. Spread some on the soil surface around plants or add a little to potting soil. Store moist leftovers in breathable paper bags where it won't go moldy.

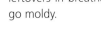

# PRUNING

Some gardeners have a "let it be" attitude with the garden. The idea is to let nature take its course, allowing plants to grow wild and free. That's cool, but not all pruning is cosmetic. Some plants actually benefit from a little haircut now and then. Cutting back excess growth allows air and light to reach remote areas of the plant, reducing problems with diseases such as powdery mildew that thrive in humid environments. Cutting back dead or diseased growth can be essential to reviving the health of a plant. Pruning also encourages more flowers and persuades plants to bush out rather than grow tall and thin.

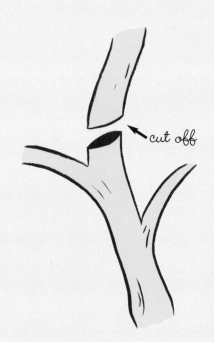

## Pinching Out

Regular pinching out of new growth of herbs such as basil gives you a bushier plant and a larger, better harvest. Most herbs taste better before the plant produces flowers—pinching out prevents flowers from forming and extends the harvest. When pinching out, remove the top of an entire stem, leaves and all, by pinching the soft growth off using your thumb and forefinger. Scissors work, too, but fingers are handier. Start doing this early in the season and continue into the fall.

## Deadheading

Removing dead flowers tricks plants into making more flowers instead of putting their energy into producing seeds. Some plants such as pansies will actually bloom continuously if deadheaded. For a tidy look, use pruners, scissors, or your fingers to cut the stem at the base rather than right under the flower head.

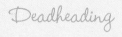

## General Pruning

Pruning is good practice when plants are weak, thin, or even too vigorous. Using a sharp pair of secateurs, make angled cuts at a spot where branches meet. New growth will emerge from there. When removing dead or diseased growth, don't hesitate to cut right back into healthy, green growth. It may seem like a lot, but your plant will regenerate soon enough. Dead parts will never magically come back to life!

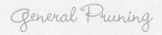
cut off

# ALL ABOUT STAKING

Ah, the wonderful and often overlooked world of staking. Staking works in oh so many ways. It helps prop up veggie plants like tomatoes, beans, and peppers that collapse under their own weight. It also keeps plants off the ground where they are handy for slugs, snails, and other low-down creepy crawlies. Staking container-grown trailing plants can keep the foliage off the hot deck and save precious space.

Don't waste your money on flimsy store-bought tomato cages, peony rings, and other overpriced contraptions. It's easier, cheaper, and craftier to use scrap materials like leftover wood, pruned branches and twigs, cheap bamboo poles, or metal rods from the hardware store. Use pantyhose (nice and stretchy), torn T-shirts (use green shirts to match plants or hot pink to contrast), or bundles of dollar-store jute or butcher's twine to secure stems in place.

*single stake*

## Single Stakes

Single stakes are simply that, single metal or wood poles set into the ground to support one branch or stem. It is the best support for Asiatic lilies and other single-stemmed plants that flop under the weight of their heavy flowers. You can also single-stake tomatoes, peppers, and trees.

## Tripod

This structure is perfect for peas, sweet peas, runner beans, and a host of climbing perennials. It is my favorite method for tomatoes and cucumbers in containers because it's secure against winds that are like tornados on exposed balconies. It is also incredibly easy to construct and take apart at the end of the growing season. Simply cut the strings and store your poles until next year.

To build:

**1.** Set three bamboo poles deeply into the soil at an equal distance around the edge of the container.

**2.** Tie a piece of twine a few inches down from the top of one pole and wrap the twine around the other poles, pulling them tightly together at the top, like a teepee.

**3.** Plant climbers like peas and beans at the base of each stake. In a large space, tomatoes can be planted one per stake, but in a small container set one plant in the center of the tepee.

*tripod stake*

## Pea Staking

This is an artfully lazy method using twiggy branches pruned from trees or bushes. It's best for trailers (traditionally peas) or other plants with thin, flimsy stems. All you have to do is find branches with lots of twiggy ends. Set them in the ground around your plant while it is still small. The branches can be set close enough so that the twiggy ends interconnect. Eventually your plant stems will grow up among the twigs where they will be supported in an upright position.

## Corraling

Create a corral using stakes and string. You can use purchased bamboo poles or found branches. Set several stakes around the perimeter of your plant. Tie string to one stake and wrap from stake to stake encircling the entire plant, holding it in place with the string.

## Crisscross Screen

Build this trellis when you want to create a screen of climbers such as beans, passionflower, or clematis.

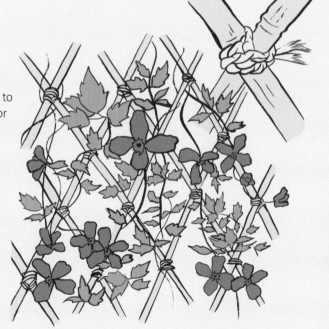

**To build:**

**1.** Push a bamboo pole into the soil at a 60-degree angle.

**2.** Push three or four more poles into the soil at the same angle in a row, spacing them 5 to 10 inches apart.

**3.** Now push an equal number of stakes into the soil starting from the opposite direction. They should be inserted at the same 60-degree angle. Your poles will cross one another, creating X shapes.

**4.** Tie a string or piece of twine at each point where two poles cross.

# WEEDS

What makes a weed a weed is really a matter of perspective. A weed is any plant that is growing where you don't want it—a displaced plant. Some weeds are invasive plants, opportunists that simply take off and take over under the right conditions.

But most weeds suffer from a bad rap. Quite a few of the weeds in your garden are probably edible or even medicinal. Some invasive plants, including horsetail and nettle, are rich in minerals and can be harvested and used as fertilizer teas. Weeds with deep tap-roots, such as dandelions, cultivate the soil and pull minerals up to the surface. You can also use weeds as signposts to identify the type of soil in your garden (see "Reading Weeds," page 45).

Weeds are nature's way to cover bare soil. After all, weeds prevent erosion by holding soil and minerals in place. Get to know the weeds in your area so you can put them to use for rather than against you. If they become a problem, pull up weeds and use a thick mulch to keep them from coming back. Layer several pieces of newspaper over the area and cover with a heavy mulch such as compost or wood shavings to hold it all in place (see page 52 for mulching tips). To completely eradicate weeds from an area, lay thick plastic down and hold in place with rocks for several weeks. The weeds will bake under the plastic!

### TIP: WEED AFTER IT RAINS.

With the soil damp and loose, it's a breeze to pull out those weeds.

## Safe Organic Herbicides

When mulching and hand-picking aren't an option, try these recipes to make safe herbicides that won't harm humans or pets.

* **Vinegar and salt** is great for places where you won't be growing anything in the near future. Fill a spray bottle with vinegar, mix in a tablespoon of salt and spray directly on plants.

* To remove young plants, pour **boiling water** directly on them. Just be careful to avoid plants that you don't want to damage.

* Pour **Coca-Cola** on the cracks in the sidewalk to kill weeds. Apply repeatedly when the sun is bright and hot for added effect. It's sticky, but within a week the weeds will be dead.

* Spray a 1:1:10 mix of **gin, apple cider vinegar, and water** on your weeds, being careful to avoid other plants.

* **Sunflower shells** make a great herbicide that can prevent seedlings from sprouting. A thick layer of empty shells (taken from below a bird feeder) will suppress weed growth.

* Hire a **herd of goats or a flock of geese** to come in and eat your weeds away. For real!

# HERE COMES TROUBLE

## GARDENING WITH INSECTS

Garden pests are as inevitable as another Rolling Stones farewell tour. At some point in your gardening life you will encounter creepy crawlies eating your tomatoes or discover an alien bug invasion taking over your flower bed.

When it comes to putting the kibosh on pests, every gardener has two options: the tried-and-true organic methods from before the days of chemicals, or chemicals. I stay away from chemical pesticides and herbicides for the typical reasons: they're dangerous to people and bad for the environment. Chemicals that are sprayed on plants rub off onto the skin and are ingested by curious and unsuspecting creatures (including children, pets, and wildlife). And when you spray, the chemical doesn't magically disappear; it finds its way into the soil, the groundwater, and finally into your faucet.

If that isn't enough to convince you to get off the chemical addiction, consider this: pesticides are counterproductive in the garden and can create more work rather than less. Most chemicals are not "smart bombs"—they will kill off all insects in the garden, both the good and the bad. The fact is, most insects are harmless and even helpful—your plants need them! Insects help pollinate your veggies, dig up the soil, aid decomposition of plant debris, and occasionally even look pretty.

Like yin and yang and chips and dip, the natural world requires balance. Where there are sap-sucking insects there are also predatory insects to feed on them. Sometimes in an effort to kill off pests, a gardener inadvertently creates a cozy predator-free environment that plant-eating insects happily move into. Before you know it, your garden will be filled with plant-eating bugs peacefully frolicking and stuffing their bellies without the fear of being eaten. This isn't limited to chemical sprays. Even organic, all-natural sprays can kill off populations of good bugs. If you must use a spray, even a "natural" one, be sure to use it cautiously and sparingly.

The way to stay off the spray is by building a healthy, strong, pest-resistant garden.

# GOOD BUGS, BAD BUGS

Knowing which insects do positive work in your garden and which are up to no good is the first step toward natural pest control. With a little knowledge under your garden belt, you can become the mad genius behind a battle of good vs. evil in your garden.

## THE GOOD

### Bees and Wasps

While you may be afraid of stings, bees and wasps are good insects to have hanging out in your garden. Bees are excellent pollinators and won't sting unless you bother them. Wasps are often lured into the garden by pollen but stick around to prey on harmful flies and insects. There are even a few types known as parasitic wasps (braconid and ichneumon) that take things to another level by laying their eggs in insect pests such as aphids and caterpillars. The wasp larvae then develop inside the host insect, which is gross, but good news for your garden.
**To attract:** Grow pollen-heavy flowering plants such as dill, yarrow, and anise-hyssop.

ground beetle

### Ground Beetles

Not all beetles are harmful plant munchers. Despite its ugly mug, the ground beetle is a small, harmless black beetle that lives in crevices underneath rocks and mulch. Learn to love them because they're in your garden feasting on slugs, Colorado potato beetle larvae, and caterpillars. Even the ground beetle larvae get in on the action as efficient caterpillar killers.
**To attract:** Lay down mulch or paving stones.

lacewing

### Lacewing

Lacewings are beautifully delicate garden predators with green bodies and lacy wings. Their larvae are voracious aphid eaters (hence the common name aphid lions) but will also feast on soft-bodied insects, including mealybugs, red spider mites, thrips, and other insect eggs and larvae.
**To attract:** Grow plants such as yarrow, angelica, tansy, or fennel.

## Ladybug

Both lady beetle larvae and adults are famous for their ability to devour a population of aphids, and they won't pass up a dinner of mealybugs or spider mites either. Not all ladybugs are red with black spots. Some are all black, black with red spots, or yellow/orange with spots. Larvae look like little, bumpy-skinned alligators and come in brown, black, or black with reddish markings. Ladybugs can be purchased for release in the garden. That sounds like a good idea, but getting the released ladybugs to stick around is difficult, making this an ineffective and pricey way to keep your pests in check.

**To attract:** Plant flowers heavy with pollen and nectar such as yarrow. Allow herbs like basil or dill to produce flowers.

ladybug

## Praying Mantid (Mantis)

Mantids will eat just about anything (including one another) and unfortunately that includes other beneficial insects. Still, they are very aggressive predators that do a great job in the garden.

**To attract:** Encourage them to take up residence and lay egg cases in your garden for next year's batch by leaving some native plants unpruned in the garden over the winter.

## Spiders

They might give you the willies, but they're great allies in the garden. Spiders feast on all sorts of insect pests but, unfortunately, they don't discriminate and will eat both the good and the bad.

**To attract:** If there is prey, they will come, so you don't need to sweat it.

ladybug larva

## THE BAD

### Ants

Ants won't cause much damage to plants on their own, but if you see a crowd of them hanging out on your plants, it is important to check up on who they're partying with. Ants will actually farm soft-bodied insects such as aphids and scale like miniature cows, milking them for their sweet honeydew secretions. In exchange, ants protect these vulnerable insects from predators. If you see ants mingling with the nasties, leave the ants and go after their troublesome friends instead.

**To combat:** Try spreading some cucumber peels around the base of infested plants. Alternately, apply Vaseline to the base of plant stems to keep ants off.

## Aphids

The granddaddy of insect garden pests. Anyone who has fought in a battle of the aphids knows far too much about the havoc aphids can create in short time. Aphids are notoriously resilient, in part because they are born pregnant! And that's just creepy.

Aphids come in a rainbow of colors from green to gray to red. Some have wings and some are wingless. Either way the damage is the same—they suck sap from tender plant parts and flowers, curling and weakening new growth. Aphids can also transmit viruses between plants and encourage sooty mold that grows on their honeydew secretions.

**To combat:** Attract aphid predators such as ladybugs, lacewings, hoverflies, parasitic wasps, or praying mantids to your garden by growing the plants they love. As a last resort, spray with garlic, citrus, or insecticidal soap (see page 116 for recipes).

**To combat:** Plant chives, basil, catnip, yarrow, and strong mints nearby. Aphids are attracted to the color yellow. Grow yellow nasturtiums nearby to attract aphids away from prized plants.

*aphid*

## Caterpillars

All sorts of moths and butterflies begin life as caterpillars. As adults they can be great allies by pollinating flowers in your garden. However, caterpillars have an insatiable appetite and can eat a busload of greenery overnight. If you can, identify caterpillars before killing them. Some may be the young of important or endangered species that might warrant a little sacrifice on your part.

*caterpillar*

## Herbal Buzz Spray

Combine caffeine with naturally insect-repellent herbs and you get an all-organic bug-chasing spritz that has the power to clear aphids off infested plants. Insect repellent herbs include yarrow, tansy, pennyroyal, thyme, lavender, rue, catnip, and artemisia.

**1.** In a bowl or old yogurt container, mix together 1 cup of one or more of the above fresh herbs (include leaves, flowers, and stems), 2 tablespoons used coffee grounds, and 2 cups of water.

**2.** Allow to steep for 24 hours. Place in the sun for a stronger infusion.

**3.** Strain and pour into a spray bottle.

**4.** Spray on infested plants. Be sure to get the undersides of leaves where bugs are hiding. Spray can be kept for a few weeks.

*Try adding insecticidal soap or castile soap for extra power.*

**To combat:** Pluck them by hand from plants. Caterpillars hang out on the underside of leaves. Some come out only at night. If you see damage without the culprit, check your plants after the sun has gone down. A bacterial spray with *Bacillus thuringiensis,* found at most garden centers, can be used as a last-ditch control.

## Colorado Potato Beetles

As you can probably guess, this type of beetle is a pest to members of the potato family (nightshades), including eggplant, tomato, and peppers. They are round and pudgy with red heads and black and yellow stripes down their backs. Larvae live in the soil, feeding on roots, while adult beetles chew through leaves.

**To combat:** Luckily, Colorado potato beetles are easy to catch. To curb an infestation, set a bucket of soapy water under the infested plant, then gently shake the plant. The beetles will fall right into the water and drown. Laying mulch around plants will attract the ground beetles that prey on Colorado potato beetle larvae. Mulches and row covers will also prevent adults from emerging from the soil in spring.

To repel them, surround plants with catnip, tansy, garlic, or yarrow.

colorado potato beetle

## Cucumber Beetles

Cucumber beetles are black and yellow beetles with oval bodies that are either striped or spotted. They like to eat holes into the leaves and roots of cucumbers, corn, and members of the squash family. They can also add to the damage by transmitting bacterial viruses between plants.

**To combat:** Predators such as ladybugs, parasitic wasps, and soldier beetles will help kick cucumber beetles to the curb. Apply neem (see page 114) to the soil to kill larvae and mulch thickly to prevent adults from emerging.

cucumber beetle

beetle eggs

## Cutworms

Cutworms are larvae of moths that live in the top inch of the soil. They come out at night to feast on the tender stems of newly planted seedlings. They literally cut stems in two, causing permanent destruction.

**To combat:** To keep cutworms from tearing into newly planted vegetable seedlings, create a barrier using a toilet roll tube or a collar cut from a plastic bottle (see page 113 for details).

You can purchase parasitic nematodes that will kill the worms in the soil. Ground beetles love a cutworm meal. Plant low-growing, permanent ground cover or apply mulch to attract the ground beetles to your garden.

## Flea Beetles

Flea beetles are tiny black or brown beetles that speckle the leaves of your edible greens with tiny holes (called "shotgun"). Although you're likely to be left with a smaller harvest, it's not tragic because you can still eat shotgun leaves.

**To combat:** Flea beetles are quick jumpers and difficult to catch. You can try spraying with catnip tea, but the answer here is prevention rather than hand-picking.

Since they don't like shade or moist habitats, apply mulch and water well to prevent dry conditions and to encourage predaceous ground beetles. Also try interplanting greens underneath taller plants where they will be in the shade.

leafhopper

## Leafhoppers

Leafhoppers are sort of cute, but they can do quite a bit of damage in the garden. As they hop about your veggies sucking sap from the leaves, they leave behind toxic saliva that burns delicate foliage. Even if you don't see any leafhoppers, their presence can be identified by curled leaf tips and edges that are crispy brown or appear burned (called "hopperburn").

**To combat:** Attract parasitic wasps to the garden, or spray infected plants with Herbal Buzz Spray (page 105). Leafhoppers hate geraniums—place pots of them around the garden or harvest the leaves for Herbal Buzz Spray.

## Leafminers

Leafminers are the larvae of a small fly that live within leaves, carving tunnels as they feed on plant tissue. They particularly like columbine and leafy greens such as swiss chard. Remove and destroy infected leaves and apply neem. It is the best organic defense against them as it is taken up into the plant, making the leaves unpalatable to the larvae.

**To combat:** Parasitic wasps in the garden will take care of them.

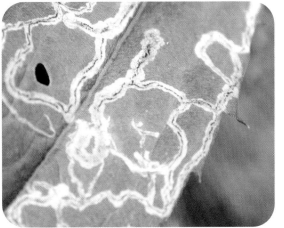

leafminer trail

## Slugs and Snails

You know them by their trail of slime. Slugs and snails love to chew on leaves and especially prefer to get their slime on by hangin' out on plants that grow in moist, shady locations. Even if you can't see them during the day, you can often recognize the damage and see their slime trails in the cold light of morning. These trails actually act like road maps alerting other slugs to the goods!

**To combat:** Your best bet is to set up barriers and traps (see Pest Prophylactics, page 112). Enlist the help of natural predators, including ground beetles, lizards, toads, and snakes, to do the nasty work for you.

## Sowbugs

Generally a few in the garden isn't a big deal because sowbugs mostly eat decaying plant matter. However, a squirming pile of sowbugs, aka pillbugs, can be a revolting sight. Sowbugs prefer moist, shady areas and especially love to congregate underneath logs, rocks, and container saucers.

**To combat:** If you find them eating young seedlings, sprinkle the area with diatomaceous earth (see page 114).

## SIX PEST-PROTECTION POINTERS

If your garden is under attack by creepy crawlies, you may need to resort to pest control products. Garden stores sell an arsenal of chemical pesticides, but if you're going organic, the products and concoctions below will do the trick. Remember that even natural products can be harmful in concentrated amounts. Organic sprays will harm beneficial insects, too, so be certain you are attacking a harmful pest, not an invited guest.

＊ **Healthy Soil, Healthy Plants**—Healthy plants are naturally pest-resistant and actually prevent infestations all on their own. Build up your soil and keep your plants healthy and strong.

＊ **Remove Diseased Plants**—Insects are generally attracted to weak and diseased plants, not healthy ones. If you're losing the battle with one crop, remove it for the good of the whole garden. It hurts to dig up and toss plants, but in this case it's a worthwhile sacrifice.

*slug damag*

*snail*

* **Grow Pest-Resistant Plants**—Some plants are finicky softies that seem prone to all sorts of problems. Tea roses are a classic example. Skip those and instead grow plants that are tough or pest-resistant. The most pest-resistant plants tend to be native to your area since they are well adapted to local conditions.

* **Don't Overfertilize**—Too much fertilizer can actually weaken plants. Excess nitrogen especially can promote the soft, tender growth that sap-sucking aphids adore. Ease up on the fertilizer!

* **Keep Your Tools Clean**—Good sanitation will prevent the spread of disease, which will prevent insect infestations.

* **Don't Grow a Monoculture**—Rather than growing several of one type of veggie in straight, uniform rows, interplant flowers and herbs to attract beneficial insects and confuse bad bugs. Organized chaos is the new garden plan!

## SEND IN THE TROOPS

Dig this: instead of additives and chemicals, plants themselves can be used in a variety of ways to control pests.

* Nectar-heavy flowers attract beneficial insects to the garden, ensuring an army of defenders against harmful insects. Dill, parsley, Queen Anne's lace, carrots, mints, and chamomile lure beneficial insects such as ladybugs and bumblebees to your garden (see sidebar for more plant options). Grow them around or near plants that attract harmful insects such as aphids and flea beetles. Your insect defense squad will keep the plant-eating population in check for you.

* Some plants will actually repel pest insects and some animals. Surround your veggies with garlic or onion to confuse insect pests. Alternatively, grow plants that contain natural repellents nearby. Lavender, yarrow, tansy, rue, catnip, and artemisia all have repellents built right in.

* Other plants have what it takes to attract specific insect pests. Many insects love yellow flowers or plants with tender, sappy foliage. Grow nasturtiums, columbine, and mustards as decoy traps to lure sap-sucking pests away from the good stuff. Once a population has moved in, remove and destroy the infested plant.

## Plants That Attract Beneficial Insects

Grow these plants to attract pollinating and beneficial insects to your garden.

* Alyssum (*Lobularia maritima*)
* Angelica (*Angelica* species)
* Basil (try sacred basil, *Ocimum sanctum*)
* Borage (*Borago officinalis*)
* Butterfly bush (*Buddleja davidii*)
* Butterfly weed (*Asclepias tuberosa*)
* Calendula (*Calendula officinalis*)
* Chamomile (*Chamaemilum nobile*)
* Dill (*Antheum graveolens*)
* Feverfew (*Tanacetum parthenium*)
* Goldenrod (*Solidago* species)
* Heather (*Calluna vulgaris*)
* Mint (*Mentha* species)
* Parsley (*Petroselinum crispum*)
* Portulaca (*Portulaca grandiflora*)
* Queen Anne's lace (*Daucus carota*)
* Rugosa roses (*Rosa rugosa*)
* Sweet William (*Dianthus barbatus*)
* Tansy (*Tanacetum vulgare*)
* Yarrow (*Achillea millefolium*)

# PLANTS THAT EAT MEAT

Carnivorous plants are not just exotic fairy-tale creatures that eat monkeys and barbershop employees. All sorts of curiously savage plants are munching on insects right this minute, even in the wilds of New Jersey. With minimal fuss, you can set up a miniature carnivorous bog container in your own backyard or on your deck and unleash insect-eating plants on the creepy crawlies inhabiting your garden.

## CHOOSING A CONTAINER

Your bog can be as simple as one plant in a teacup or as complex as a group of carnivorous and noncarnivorous bog plants in a big ol' bathtub. Carnivores come in all shapes and sizes, from teeny sundews to majestic trumpet pitchers. You can use any sealed container, including salad bowls and groovy old Crock-Pots, for your bog. If your container does have drainage holes, set it inside a shallow dish of water.

## GROWING

**Water**—When it comes to water, CPs are a finicky crew. With some variation, the one thing most have in common is a love of wet, boglike conditions. Keep the soil moist, but allow water levels to fluctuate between soaking and damp, but never dry.

Here's where it gets tricky. Carnivores do not like hard water or any water with dissolved mineral salt content. This means that Seymour will die if he drinks tap water, spring water, or mineral water. Opt instead for rainwater or reverse-osmosis water. This sounds like a drag. But it's so worth it when you see your plant eating the mosquito that's been driving you nuts all afternoon.

**Light**—Most carnivores do well in bright areas.

**Fertilizing**—For the most part, carnivorous plants living outside will happily catch an abundance of insect prey and do not require hand-feeding. Although it does make a great party trick!

### Mix It Up

Make your bog look superfly by adding ornamental bog grasses and reeds. Try:
* Corkscrew rush (*Juncus effusus* 'Spiralis')
* Horsetail (*Equisetum hyemale*)
* Spike rush (*Eleocharis montevidensis*)
* Square rush (*Eleocharis quadrangulata*)
* Yellow-eyed grass (*Xyris baldwiniana*)

## PLANTS TO TRY

### Cold Climates

These carnivorous plants are easy to grow and can tough it out through a real winter. They actually require a cool or cold dormant period and are not ideal for warm climates. If you cannot provide an outdoor cold period, you can fake it by refrigerating them in plastic baggies for the suggested dormancy length.

* Butterwort, aka "pings" (*Pinguicula vulgaris, P. grandiflora, P. longifolia*)
* Purple pitcher (*Sarracenia purpurea*)—Can handle a deep freeze.
* Sundew (*Drosera filiformis, D. linearis, D. rotundifolia, D. anglica*)—Sundews are annuals, so be sure to collect seeds after flowering.
* Venus fly trap (*Dioneae muscipula*)—Can withstand short freezes but do better in temperate climates. Plant in a container with holes in the bottom and place a water-filled tray underneath.

### Warm Climates

These plants are also easy to grow and don't require a cold period. They aren't hardy in climates with a true winter. Unless you live in a mild climate, bring them indoors in early fall to overwinter.

* Butterwort (*Pinguicula primuliflora*)
* Sundew (*Drosera capensis, D. burmanni, D. spatulata, D. brevifolia*)
* Trumpet pitcher (*Sarracenia flava, S. alata, S. rubra, S. x 'Judith Hindle'*)

## GET SOME

As carnivorous plants are becoming the "it" plants for avant-gardeners, it's getting easier to find them in corner markets, flower shops, and nurseries. An assortment of growers across the United States and Canada will ship to your home during warm seasons. If you're adventurous (and patient), try growing from seed. To get access to an enormous collection of seeds, join a group like the International Carnivorous Plant Society (see Resources). If you are lucky enough to see a carnivorous plant growing in the wild, take a photo but leave the plant.

## MAKE YOUR OWN BOG

### You Will Need

* Bucket
* Sand (plant-safe, no herbicides)
* Peat
* Perlite
* Dust mask and/or goggles
* Water (mineral-free)
* Sealed pot or container (no holes)
* Drill and ¼-inch bit (optional)
* Rocks or gravel
* Carnivorous plants

**1.** In a bucket, mix together 1 part sand, 1 part peat, and 1 part perlite. Wear face protection to keep the dust out of your eyes and nose.

**2.** Pour lots of water into the mix and set aside until the peat has absorbed it all. Keep adding water until the peat is moist. This is an important step because dry peat will suck moisture from your plants!

**3.** To prevent your plant from drowning in a downpour and to avoid creating a breeding ground for unwanted insects, you can drill a few holes 1 inch down from the top of the pot (optional). This will help standing water drain off the surface.

**4.** Add a 1- or 2-inch layer of rocks to the bottom of your container. Fill the pot with your peaty bog mix, leaving 2 inches of space at the top.

**5.** Plant one or several carnivorous plants that are right for your climate in your new bog. And let them eat flies!

# PEST PROPHYLACTICS

The concept behind barriers and traps is simple: block insects from getting at the goods. Because they don't rely on chemicals or sprays, barriers and traps are ecologically friendly. It's super easy to assemble the following devices from stuff in your recycling bin or junk drawer and use them in your garden to keep known insect pests from making a meal of your plants.

## SLUG FUNNEL

Here's a trap that gives new meaning to the term "beer funnel." Cut a plastic bottle in half and invert the top half into the bottom half to create a funnel. Partially sink the trap into the soil near slug-infested plants. A little leftover beer poured into the bottom of the trap creates a happy ending for slugs and gardener alike.

*cut here*

## PENNIES FROM HELL

A strip of copper sheeting or wire placed around plants will give slugs and snails a shock to remember. Contact with copper zaps their slime with a mild electric shock. Pennies can also be laid around the base of plants as a barrier, but make sure to use pennies older than 1980—after the mid-1980s the content of pennies was switched from primarily copper to zinc.

## WALKING ON EGGSHELLS

The sharp edges of broken eggshells are like razor blades against the soft underbellies of hungry slugs and snails. Sounds gross, but a layer of broken shells surrounding each plant really just acts as a barrier rather than a slug death trap. No slug corpses will be on your conscience with this one.

To make a protective moat, save your eggshells in a resealable plastic bag. Once the bag is about half full, roll over it with a rolling pin or empty wine bottle to create a crunchy powder. Sprinkle a layer of shells around the base of plants that are known slug favorites. That's all it takes! Plus eggshells are a bonus soil amender.

## STICKY TRAP

A wide range of insect pests, including whitefly, fungus gnats, thrips, aphids, and flea beetles, happen to be attracted to the color yellow. You can take advantage of this predilection to attract and trap them. Make a sticky trap by coating a square of yellow poster board with petroleum jelly, molasses, or spray oil. Stake the boards with popsicle sticks and jam them into the soil. Yellow-loving insects will fly into the board and get stuck. To hang traps directly from an infested plant, attach an opened paper clip to each card like a hook. Sling the other end of the paper clip hook from a branch.

## TOILET PAPER COLLAR

Cutworms live just below the soil surface during the day, patiently waiting to chop your tomato seedlings off at the stem during the night. A simple collar surrounding the stem of your plant will keep cutworms away from your precious seedlings.

Cut the cardboard center of a toilet roll in half. Thread the tube around the plant and push it halfway into the soil. The toilet roll will disintegrate over time, so there is no need to remove it as the plant grows. Just set it and forget it!

## FOILED AGAIN

Make a hole in the center of a flat square of aluminum foil and place around the base of tender, young plants. The reflecting light confuses pests such as aphids, thrips, and beetles.

# NATURAL INSECT CONTROL PRODUCTS

If your garden is under attack by creepy crawlies, you may need to resort to pest control products. Garden stores sell an arsenal of chemical pesticides, but if you're going organic, the products and concoctions below will do the trick. Remember that even natural products can be harmful in concentrated amounts. Organic sprays will harm beneficial insects, too, so be certain you are attacking a harmful pest, not an invited guest.

## Diatomaceous Earth

This powder is made from the fossilized shells of tiny creatures called diatoms. Their microscopic sharp edges penetrate an insect's cuticle, causing it to die of dehydration. Nasty! Sprinkle diatomaceous earth around the base of plants to discourage slugs, snails, and caterpillars. The fine dust is nontoxic to mammals but incredibly irritating if inhaled. Protect yourself by wearing a dust mask while handling!

## Insecticidal Soap

Soap sprays work a lot like diatomaceous earth—they penetrate the cuticle of the insect and lead to dehydration. This type of spray works best on soft-bodied insects like aphids, whiteflies, thrips, and mealybugs but must be applied directly to the insect's body to work. Soaps can be added to other insecticidal ingredients, including herb teas, for added strength and to increase the stickiness of the mix.

If you're feeling crafty or cheap, make your own spray using nondetergent, additive-free soaps (try castile soap) diluted with water. Or you can drop the big bucks on insecticidal soap at the garden center. It's concentrated and incredibly long lasting—I've had the same bottle for several years.

## Neem Oil

Neem oil is extracted from the seeds of the neem tree, common to India. Neem oil is pretty much a miracle product. It's useful for all kinds of fungal infections and acts as an insect repellent, poison, and growth regulator (prevents insects from maturing). Neem also acts systemically—meaning it's absorbed by the plant, making the plant unpalatable to the insect pest for several weeks.

Neem is effective against a wide range of pests. It can be poured onto the soil or sprayed directly on leaves to attack eggs and larvae. Neem oil is a hot new item in a lot of garden stores. If you can't find it there, try health food stores and stores that carry beauty products from India. I purchase my neem oil at a fraction of the cost at my local Indian imports store.

## Pyrethrin

Pyrethrin is an insect nerve poison extracted from the pyrethrum daisy (*Chrysanthemum coccineum*). Aphids, cabbage loopers, codling moths, Colorado potato beetles, spider mites, thrips, whiteflies, and Mexican bean beetles are just some of the bugs susceptible to the poison. You can make your own pyrethrin spray from the dried flowers of the plant, or you can buy prepared sprays from the garden center. Check the ingredients to be sure other more harmful products have not been added.

**Caution:** Sure it comes from a plant, but this is heavy-duty stuff. It is mildly toxic to mammals and will kill some beneficial insects. It can cause allergies and skin rashes in people who suffer from hayfever, so wear protection and avoid spraying on windy days.

# KITCHEN CONCOCTIONS: PEST REPELLENTS

Try these simple recipes the next time you discover a battalion of aphids or other unwanted creepy crawlies making a meal of your future meal.

## SMELLERIFIC CITRUS PEEL SPRAY

**Victims:** Soft bodied insects such as aphids, mites, and caterpillars.

**1.** Steep the chopped orange or lemon peel overnight in the hot water.

**2.** Strain this citrus brew through a thin-meshed strainer. Be sure to capture all the particles to avoid clogging your sprayer.

**3.** Funnel the liquid into a spray bottle and you're ready to spritz.

**Nonedible Variation:** Add 1 teaspoon nondetergent soap or insecticidal soap to the mix. Not only will it aid the mix in sticking to the insect, but it will also do its own damage.

### How to Use

Be sure to test the sensitivity of your plant before launching a full-on assault. Some plants will burn when directly sprayed with citrus oil, especially in hot sun. Move your plant away from direct sun if possible and spray the underside of one leaf. Wait an hour or up to one day and then go ahead if no damage was done. You must spray the insects directly to get the job done. Indirect contact with this mild insecticide won't kick them where it hurts.

### Why It Works

Oils found in the peel of all citrus fruit act as a nerve poison that sends soft-bodied insects into a crazy fit upon contact. Of course anyone who has experienced citrus juice in the eye is also aware that it burns.

### You Will Need

* Chopped peel of one citrus fruit (orange or lemon)
* 4 cups of boiling water
* Fine strainer
* Funnel
* Spray bottle

# BAD BREATH PEPPER GARLIC SPRAY

**Victims:** All-purpose, including flea beetles, Mexican bean beetles, ants, and potato beetles. Try it on a host of insect pests, but do be aware that this spray will kill beneficial insects along with harmful ones. Some rodents will also be repelled by the hot pepper.

**1.** Steep the garlic, onion, and hot pepper overnight in boiling water.

**2.** Pour the whole mess into a blender or food processor and liquefy.

**3.** Strain through cheesecloth, coffee filter, or a fine-meshed strainer. Be sure to capture all the particles to avoid clogging your sprayer.

**4.** Funnel the liquid into a spray bottle.

**Nonedible Variation:** Add 1 teaspoon nondetergent soap or insecticidal soap to the mix. The stickiness of soap helps the mix stick to the plant longer but also smothers and dehydrates insects.

## How to Use

Thoroughly coat the leaves of the infected plant with the spray. Be sure to get the undersides and other nooks and crannies where bugs will hide. Store your mixture in the fridge to avoid the rotting smell that starts in about 2 weeks.

## Why It Works

Garlic contains a chemical that bugs loathe and that has fungicidal properties, and it also contains sulfur, which will prevent some diseases. Hot pepper contains capsicum, the stuff that burns your eyes.

## You Will Need

* 1 tablespoon hot pepper (flakes, powder, or fresh)
* 4 cups of boiling water
* 1 entire bulb of garlic
* 1 smallish onion, roughly chopped
* Blender or food processor
* Fine strainer, cheesecloth, or coffee filter
* Funnel
* Spray bottle

# ANIMAL CRITTERS

No matter where you live (barring a hermetically sealed bubble), you will always be sharing space with the local wildlife. They're certainly entitled to their space, but squirrels, raccoons, and other mammals can get into garbage and slip through open doors looking for a meal. Once you start a garden in the city, it's only a matter of time before a stealthy creature is lured into your garden hoping to get a piece of the pie. Below are a few suggestions to help you save your plants from pesky critters. But do be forewarned that what works once may not work a second time. There may come a time when you will have to accept a certain amount of loss to your friendly neighborhood squirrel.

## Birds

Birds can be an asset or a burden in a garden. They will eat all kinds of grubs, slugs, and nasties, but will also eat a whole lot of your fruit and berry harvest. Still, waking up to the sound of happy, chirping birds is a lovely way to start the day. And the arrival of an unusual bird guest in a barren urban environment can be as exciting as sighting your favorite 1970s sitcom star.

**To attract:** Put out dishes of fresh water and appropriate seed mixes in rat- and squirrel-proof feeders. Hang up a birdhouse or two.

**To control:** To keep birds off your strawberries, lay mesh over the patch or make a wire cloche for potted plants (see page 122).

**To repel:** Construct a shiny noisemaker using cut-up pieces of foil pie tins hung from string. Attach near plants the birds particularly love to scare them away.

## Squirrels

Squirrels are pesky city critters that love to get into everything. Squirrels like to dig. I'm not sure if they're looking for buried food or just having fun, but they go nuts digging for a few months between spring and summer. Unfortunately, this is the time when you will be setting out and establishing young seedlings. Oftentimes they won't eat the seedlings, they'll just keep digging them up until the poor plants can't take it anymore, wilt, and die. Squirrels also seem to prefer digging in freshly cultivated soil over hard, compacted soil.

## Stink Them Out

You can spritz homemade repellent sprays or store-bought formulas with names like Critter-Ridder onto areas where critters forage and dig. A general all-purpose spray made of hot pepper flakes will deter pests but can be cruel if it gets into their eyes. Sprays do the job directly after application, but you'll need to reapply regularly and after rain.

* Bloodmeal sprinkled on the soil around plants will keep away annoying critters, including your neighbors—the stuff stinks! It does double duty as a fertilizer.

* Burn frankincense to keep away raccoons, cats, and squirrels. They hate the strong smell.

* Strong-smelling herbs such as mint will deter some critters, including rats.

**To control:** Your best mode of defense is protection. Surround newly planted seedlings and seeds with a cloche cut from a pop bottle (see Protecting Your Babies, page 76).

## Raccoons

Raccoons are nighttime culprits that go for easy sources of food. In addition to garbage, they are likely to make a beeline for that tasty tomato just ripening on the vine.

**To control:** Keep oils, meat, and other smelly, slow-composting ingredients out of the compost pile. Arrange plants and containers so that appealing plants are protected behind prickly foliage like cucumbers or prickly pear cactus.

## Rats and Mice

Rats and mice can do a bit of damage in the garden but for the most part their peskiness is more about the gross-out factor. City rats are quite unlike their cute domestic cousins. Discovering a dog-sized rat nibbling on your veggie crop or Ben nesting behind the bushes is kind of creepy.

**To control:** The best defense is to go on the offense. Keep your compost bin covered and do not add meat or oils to the pile.

**To repel:** Get a cat or lure neighborhood cats to your garden. You can also attract wild predators such as bats by installing a bat house. Whatever you do, do not grow valerian. Rats love it!

## Cats

I love my cat. I even love wandering neighborhood cats that find my garden and decide to hang out. Cats act as garden security guards, chasing away squirrels, rats, and mice. Turds left on the garden will also keep critters at bay when the cat's away. What I do not like are feline chew marks on beloved plants or finding poo surprises in planter boxes.

**To repel:** Plant cat-repellent plants that have a smell cats hate, such as scaredy cat plant (*Coleus canina*), or lay chopped citrus peels or pinecones around the garden. You can spray planters with cat deterrent spray. Or hide out with a water-filled squirt gun and wait to startle offending cats.

**To control:** If you can't beat 'em, provide your cat with its own space and plant an attractive cat garden that will keep kitty off your beloved plants. Once your cat has established a habit of going to its own plants, it will stay off yours (see Cat Garden, on the next page).

# CAT GARDEN

Nothing is more serene than working the garden on a summer day with your best feline friend lazing in the sun beside you. Until Fluffy gets a hankering to munch on some fresh greens! Of course, she'll pass up all the cheap annuals and head straight for an expensive new purchase or your fanciest flower.

One way to keep kitty off the goods is to drum up some dazzle camouflage and distract her with greener, tastier pastures. There's a wide, wide world of plants out there that cats can't resist. Create a mixed container with some of the cat-enticing plants listed below and set it away from other plants. With her own private Idaho filled with irresistible treats, your cat won't be tempted by your prized veggies and ornamentals.

## KITTY HERBS

### Catnip (Nepeta cataria)

This is, of course, the quintessential cat enticer. Plant regular catnip or lemon catnip (*Nepeta cataria ssp. citriodora* 'Lemony') in your garden and Fluffy will go no farther. But, believe it or not, some cats don't "do" catnip. If your cat doesn't go for it, you can always use it as a calming herb tea for humans (see page 143). **Grow it**—Catnip is a tough-as-nails plant that can stand some neglect. Give it good, rich soil and prune off excess leaves during periods of high humidity to prevent a breakout of powdery mildew.

### Persian Catmint (Nepeta x faassenii)

My cat, Voltron, Defender of the Universe, goes crazy for this stuff and loves to writhe around in the little pieces I pick for her. This hardy perennial has gorgeous, sweetly aromatic flowers that are usually blue but also come in lavender, pink, and white.
**Grow it**—It's as easy to grow as regular catnip, but it's less invasive and doesn't mind some drought now and then.

## Plants That Are Toxic to Cats

Most cats know to stay away from plants that will make them sick. But if you have an especially curious kitty, it's best not to tempt him with:

* Bleeding heart
* Daffodil
* Datura
* Foxglove
* Hydrangea
* Ivy
* Marigold
* Morning glory
* Peony
* Snowdrop
* Tiger lily
* Tomato

## Valerian (*Valeriana officinalis*)

Valerian is well known as a human sedative, but it has an opposite, cuckoo, effect on some cats. Plant some in your garden and see if your cat goes wild for it. If you live in the city, though, definitely stay away from this herb. Rats love it as much as cats do!

**Grow it**—Like most herbs, valerian does well in full sun with rich soil and a fair amount of root space. Grow in containers that are at least 6 inches across.

## GRASSES

### "Cat Grass"

Cats love to munch on almost any kind of grass. The stuff you see in pet stores labeled "cat grass" is most likely one of three things: wheat, rye, or oats, or a combination thereof. Don't let the fancy label and kits fool ya: this stuff is easy to grow on your own.

**Grow it**—Fill a container three-quarters full with potting soil. Toss in a layer of seeds and cover with a half inch of soil. Water and set in a dark location for a few days. Once sprouts show on the soil surface, place the container in a sunny spot and let your kitty haven grow.

### Ornamental Grass

Now that we've debunked the myth of "cat grass," why not try growing a fancy grass container that looks beautiful and your cats will love? A few cat-safe ornamentals include blue fescue (*Festuca glauca*), purple fountain grass (*Pennisetum setaceum*), sweetgrass (*Hierochloe odorata*), white-striped ribbon grass, also known as reed canarygrass (*Phalaris arundinacea*), and tufted sedge (*Carex elata*). The 'Bowles Golden' variety is gorgeous.

**Grow it**—There's a good-looking grass plant for any environment, from dry to marshy. Choose a plant that best suits your conditions. To save time, buy or acquire ornamentals as transplants. Most grasses spread like a skin rash, so friends and neighbors will happily give chunks away.

### Lemongrass (*Cymbopogon citratus*)

My cat loves lemongrass with such intense fervor she would crawl over a mountain of prickly pear cactus and an ocean of Vicks VapoRub if a blade of delicious lemongrass awaited her on the other side. Try it out. It's okay if your cat doesn't love it like Voltron does—you can add it to spring rolls and Asian-inspired soups.

**Grow it**—Lemongrass is an easy-to-grow container herb that likes it sunny and moist. It will not survive cold winters outdoors, so bring the plant inside when the temperature drops.

### Low-Tech Cat Repellents

* Sprinkle citrus peels and cayenne pepper on the soil
* Spray vinegar on soil (be sure to keep off plants!)
* Apply Vicks VapoRub to the edges of pots or garden borders

Handy plant repellents include lavender, scaredy-cat (*Coleus canina*), rue, and lemon thyme.

### Other Herbs Your Cat Will Love

* Calamint (*Calamintha nepeta*) aka lesser calamint
* Cat thyme (*Teucrium marum*)
* Silver vine (*Actinidia polygama*)

# CHICKEN WIRE CLOCHE

Even a sweet, cheerful songbird can become the lurking menace that stands between you and your luscious, about-to-burst strawberries. A cloche is a handy barrier against birds, squirrels, cats, and other pesky garden raiders. It can be placed in the garden or set over pots of greens, cabbages, and other enticing edibles. Build this objet d'art from chicken wire and protect your bounty in style.

## You Will Need

- Protective work gloves
- Wire cutters
- Fine-mesh chicken wire
- Pliers
- Medium-gauge rustproof wire (or butcher's cord)

**1.** Wearing your protective work gloves, use wire cutters to cut a piece of chicken wire approximately 20 inches by 20 inches. Larger pots will require added width. Measure the circumference of your plant or pot before you cut to be sure it will fit.

**2.** Roll the wire to create a tube shape. Chicken wire often comes in a roll, so follow the direction of the roll.

**3.** Using your pliers, join the ends of the tube together by twisting the cut ends around each other until secure.

step 3

**4.** Stand your tube upright and squeeze the top of the tube to form a cone. Continue squeezing approximately 7 inches down the length of the tube. Your cone should be tight at the top, gradually flaring out at the bottom.

**5.** Secure your cone shape by winding the wire around the top of the cloche.

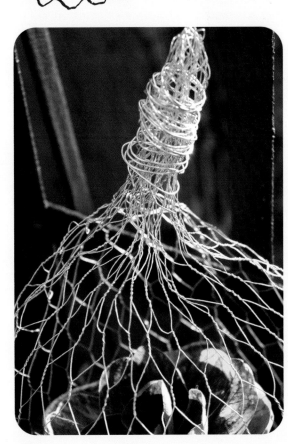

*step 4*

*step 5*

*Safety hint: Crimp all loose wire ends back with a pair of pliers to avoid poking yourself or garden guests on sharp wire points.*

# DISEASES

Just when your garden is cruising along like the *Love Boat* on Saturday night, you discover some strange white stuff on your once happy hyacinth. What's going on? Disease. Turns out that plants get rocked by illness just like we do.

Your first reaction to moldy-looking leaves or a newly dying plant might be to grab a bottle and start spaying. But before you get nuts with the sprays, remember that the presence of disease is often the sign of a cultural problem in the garden. Usually disease shows that the plant itself isn't getting what it needs (light, water, nutrition, air circulation) or it's getting too much! Look closer at the conditions your plant is growing in to figure out what isn't quite right. Disease provides an opportunity to learn more about your garden.

To stay off the spray, practice a good defense in your garden:

✴ **Keep It Tidy**—Don't let diseased leaves sit around in the soil. Search and destroy!

✴ **Prune, Prune, Prune**—Most mildews and fungal diseases thrive in humid, warm environments like the locker room at the gym. Think nasty gym socks! Pruning increases air circulation around the leaves, providing a breath of fresh air.

✴ **Clean Your Tools**—Just like someone with a cold who spreads germs by reaching into a bowl of bar peanuts, dirty tools spread diseases from one plant to another.

✴ **Water the Soil, Not the Leaves**—Disease strikes when plants have too much humidity around the leaves. Try not to water plant leaves—they can take hours to dry. If you do water the leaves, do it early in the day so they can dry out before nightfall.

✴ **Build Healthy Soil**—Healthy soil equals healthy plants equals stronger disease resistance.

✴ **Think Ahead**—You can always count on powdery mildew to break out on your zinnias when the temperature rises. Apply foliar feeds, stinky teas, or milk to plants that are known to be disease-intolerant before the problem strikes.

## Another Reason to Stop Smoking

Tobacco mosaic virus is a common viral enemy of plants in the nightshade family—most especially tomatoes. The virus can be transmitted from tobacco. To prevent the virus, avoid smoking cigarettes around tomato plants. Wash your hands after smoking and before handling plants.

# WHAT AILS THEM: COMMON PLANT DISEASES

## Blossom-End Rot

Blossom-end rot frequently occurs in tomatoes and shows as a dark, watery spot on the blossom end (usually the bottom) of the fruit.

**Cause:** It's the result of a calcium deficiency, but often the problem isn't a lack of calcium in the soil, but a lack of water to transport calcium through the plant efficiently. This is most common in container-grown plants, which dry out more frequently.

**Solution:** To avoid, keep the soil evenly moist. Even containers can use a little mulch! Add crushed eggshell to the soil as calcium mulch for good measure. Nothing can be done to fix diseased fruit. Pick it and cut off the bad parts. However, if you solve the problem quickly, your next bunch of fruit should turn out fine.

## Damping Off

If your seedlings' stems are rotting and they're toppling over, then you've got the devastating fugal disease called damping off.

**Cause:** Damping off is fungal rot encouraged by excessive watering, soil that isn't sterile, lack of air circulation, or super-wet soil.

**Solution:** Water seedlings from the bottom to prevent stem rot. Sprinkling a layer of grit or sand on the soil surface can sometimes help keep stems dry at the soil line. You can also try watering with a weak chamomile tea or sprinkling a light layer of cinnamon powder on the soil surface—both cinnamon and chamomile are antifungals. Some gardeners swear by a layer of finely powdered sphagnum moss on the soil surface to deter the disease.

## Blight & Wilt

Blights and wilts are fungal diseases that commonly affect crops in the nightshade family (tomatoes, potatoes, peppers) as well as the squash family, raspberries, and strawberries. Blights first appear as brown spots on the lower leaves that spread from the center. Heavily infected leaves eventually drop to the ground. Wilts look just like they sound: leaves and stems wilt when there seems to be no apparent reason why. Leaves eventually turn from yellow to brown and finally drop off.

**Cause:** Verticillium wilt is common in cooler, temperate climates, while fusarium wilt tends toward warmer regions. Climate can really work against you in these cases, so prepare ahead for these conditions by taking preventative measures.

**Solution:** Start out on a good foot and grow plants labeled as disease resistant. Milk or compost tea sprayed onto leaves and foliage early in the season can act as a preventative (see Spilt Milk, on page 128). Fungal diseases overwinter in the garden on infected plant matter that has been left behind. Act fast and remove infected plants before they spread. Don't leave any stray leaves or fruit behind and don't compost them!

## Powdery Mildew

Powdery mildew is a fungal disease that looks like a filmy layer of white powder that has been sprinkled on the leaves of an infected plant. As the disease spreads, leaves deteriorate and die.

**Cause:** This disease is encouraged by high humidity and poor air circulation. Some plants just can't seem to avoid a bout of powdery mildew during the hot, humid days of summer.

**Solution:** The best plan is to know which plants are susceptible and to prepare your defenses as the summer heats up. Powdery mildew commonly affects catnip, zinnia, bee balm (*Monarda*), sage, and roses. Prune excess foliage to open up air circulation and spray plants with a 50:50 milk-to-water solution or the Powdery Mildew Spray on page 129.

## Rust

This fungal disease looks like it sounds: the foliage becomes spotted with rusty-looking pocks.

**Cause:** Bad air circulation and high humidity around the leaves is often the culprit.

**Solution:** Avoid wetting leaves when watering. Sulfur spray or dust is the common store-bought control, but it's moderately toxic to animals, including you. Before resorting to the hard hitters, try the Anti-Rust Sweet Spray found on page 129.

# ORGANIC DISEASE REMEDIES

## Baking Soda

Also known as sodium bicarbonate, baking soda can be used as an antacid when you have a stomachache and as an antifungal in the garden. It's particularly effective against powdery mildew and roses infected with black spot. Don't dump a box of baking soda on your plants. Concoct an easy spray to get the most out of baking soda. See the recipe for Powdery Mildew Spray on page 129 for instructions.

## Garlic

It's good in pasta, as an insecticide, and as an antifungal to combat disease. Plant it near disease-prone plants or brew a strong garlic-clove tea to spray directly on fungal diseases. Use it wisely—garlic sprays will also kill beneficial insects.

## Horsetail

If you've got some taking over your yard, put it to good use. Horsetail *(Equisetum)* is high in silica and has a strong antifungal kick. Get two for the price of one by cutting back some of this invasive plant and brewing it into a tea to pour on plants suffering from fungal diseases and mildews.

## Neem

It slices, it dices, but wait, there's more! Neem oil, extracted from the seeds of a tree common to India, rocks as a powerful insecticide (see page 114) and a powerful antifungal. I love neem oil because of its all-purpose usefulness and because it really works!

## Stinky Tea

Teas made from compost or well-aged manure make excellent disease-fighting plant beverages. Not only do they fight disease but they arm the plant with the nutrition required to get strong and fight back. See "Rank Tea" on page 93 for instructions.

## Sulfur

Sulfur beats back mildews and black spot, but its main gig is to fight rust disease. Store-bought organic sulfur sprays are mildly toxic to animals, so use cautiously. Molasses is a sweet and safe source of sulphur. Your average cooking molasses has had the sulphur removed, so look for nonedible types sold at your local garden center that specifically include sulfur in the ingredients. Molasses also contains iron and trace minerals that are good for the soil and your plant. See Anti-Rust Sweet Spray on page 129 for recipe instructions.

# TROUBLESHOOTING

Is something plaguing your plant? Insect and disease outbreaks are often indications of a cultural problem. Before pulling out the big guns, go through this checklist to determine if something can be done to make a happier environment for your plant and an unhappy environment for pests.

☐ Are you overwatering? Some plants prefer marshlike conditions, while others will rot. Wet conditions can encourage disease and rot. Read up on your plants so you'll know what they prefer (see Water and Humidity, page 85).

☐ Are you underwatering? Desert natives and some Mediterranean plants prefer a little drought now and again, but even they require enough water to access nutrients from the soil. Blossom-end rot in tomatoes is often caused by underwatering. Try watering deeply but less frequently rather than small amounts regularly (see page 85).

☐ High humidity? Some diseases such as powdery mildew and rust thrive in hot, humid conditions. Prune back excess foliage to provide good air circulation around the leaves (see page 124).

☐ Root-bound? Is the container too small for your plant? Are lots of roots pushing through the bottom drainage hole? This can lead to a lack of air around the roots, a lack of nutrition, and can starve the plant of water. It's time to repot (see page 78 for more on repotting).

☐ Light—Too little or too much? Plants with silver foliage can take bright sun and heat. But not all plants recommended for full sun can tolerate really hot, exposed fire escapes and urban balconies. Even cacti and succulent plants shouldn't be thrown into full sun after a season indoors. Introduce plants to the sun slowly or they'll get seriously charred. If leaves look burned, move your plants or create shade (see Light, page 84).

☐ Underfertilizing? See "Become a Plant Whisperer" for tips on how to read nutritional deficiencies in plants (page 92).

☐ Overfertilizing? Excess nitrogen is a common problem, indicated by loads of plush green foliage and an absence of flowers or fruit. Cut back on high-nitrogen fertilizers (see page 90).

# KITCHEN CONCOCTIONS: DISEASE REMEDIES

Just open your kitchen cupboards and you'll find the ingredients for these antifungal, antiviral remedies. They're all safe enough to eat—if nasty-tasting potions are your thing. Sprays as a long-term solution are a bit dodgy, but as instant quick fixes they will prevent the spread of disease in the garden.

## SPILT MILK

Plain ol' skim milk is a fantastic virus and fungus fighter. It can be used to aid blight-infected roses or tomatoes suffering from a multitude of viral ailments. Pour a 50:50 water-and-milk mix into a spray bottle and apply directly to infected foliage. You can also work a tablespoon of powdered milk into the soil around transplants as preventative medicine.

Milk may or may not do the body good, but it will beat down plant viral and fungal diseases in their early stages.

## CHAMOMILE TEA

Next time you brew yourself a cup of tea, save the leftovers for your plants. Don't dump it down the sink; dump your cold chamomile right into your plants instead. A mild cup of chamomile tea can put the kibosh on damping off and other pernicious plant fungi. You can spray weak room-temperature tea onto the surface of your seedlings' soil as a preventative measure.

# POWDERY MILDEW SPRAY

As much as my tropicals flourish during the humid days of summer, they are a breeding ground for mildew diseases. While good air circulation around leaves will prevent an outbreak, you can cut back only so much foliage to encourage good flow during a heatwave before you've got nothing left. When the heat and humidity start to rise, use this spray as a preventative on susceptible plants, including sage, catnip, zinnias, cucumber, roses, and bee balm.

**1.** Mix together the baking soda, soap, and water. The soap helps the mix stick to the plant but is not an active ingredient.

**2.** Pour into a spray bottle and shake to combine.

**3.** Spray the mix all over your plants, including the undersides of leaves. Reapply once a week and after a rainfall.

*You Will Need*

* 1 tablespoon baking soda
* 1 tablespoon thick, nondetergent soap (castile soap, insecticidal soap, Murphy's oil soap, or Dr. Bronner's)
* 1 gallon water
* Spray bottle

# ANTI-RUST SWEET SPRAY

When your plants look like a pile of aged iron, you know you've got rust. Rust is a fungal disease that infects plants in warm, humid conditions. Sulfur, in the form of molasses, comes to the rescue! Its sticky sweetness gives gooey staying power while it gets the job done. This recipe also packs the power of milk (a fungicide) and seaweed (micronutrient-rich tonic), although it can be made without these extras.

**1.** In the bucket, mix together the molasses and powders into a thick paste.

**2.** Scoop the paste into the leg of an old pair of pantyhose and tie at the top to close. You can substitute a piece of old T-shirt or cheesecloth tied with string if you haven't worn pantyhose in the last five years.

**3.** Drop the bundle into a bucket of warm water and allow it to dissolve for a few hours. Once the mix has cooled, remove the bundle and discard.

**4.** Pour the mix into a spray bottle and apply liberally to the leaves of infected plants.

**5.** Repeat applications until new growth shows no signs of disease.

*You Will Need*

* 1 cup sulfured molasses
* 1 cup powdered milk (optional)
* 1 cup seaweed, aka kelp powder (optional)
* String
* Bucket
* 1 gallon warm water
* Old T-shirt, pantyhose, or cheesecloth

# GROWING FOOD

That first tomato is always the most thrilling! It's truly one of those Oprah moments when everything clicks, the world makes sense, and all that hard work pays off—just for one tomato that tastes like pure joy. It's the proudest moment in the life of a very small-scale farmer.

Even if you don't have a yard or much space at all, you can grow exotic produce that's tastier than grocery-store fare. Even in containers!

You can grow just about anything in a container if you give it the right care. Start out with something small and easy and work your way up to the fancy plants when you've got some confidence and experience. And of course don't let one failed attempt hold you back. What is easy for one person can be difficult for another for no reason other than luck. I can grow a killer patch of basil but after years of trying have yet to grow a really decent, succulent radish (one of the easiest crops to grow!). Give it a go, experiment, and have fun. If tomatoes don't work out, try another type or switch to peppers instead.

# CONTAINER FARMING

Any plant can grow in a container, but, conveniently, some vegetable varieties have been created specifically for container growing. Look for tags that indicate compact growth, miniature sizing, or heat and drought tolerance. The trick to growing container veggies is growing one plant per pot. Beginners are often overzealous and forget that each tiny seedling will grow to be a large plant with a demanding root system.

Try your hand with the following vegetables and remember that mistakes are part of learning.

## Corn (Zea mays)

Even in a small space, you can grow your own corn! Corn only hands out two or three cobs per plant, but a row of plants does double duty as a stylish privacy hedge on a deck, rooftop, or in the yard. Corn plants can also create shade for shorter plants in a sweltering space. Sweet corn varieties are those enormously towering plants you see in horror movies. But a few miniature types like 'Baby Blue' (aka 'Blue Jade') will thrive in containers. Popping corn varieties are on the smaller side and often produce adorable miniature cobs, too. Try an heirloom like 'Two Inch Strawberry', or a miniature like 'Tom Thumb'. The coolest part is harvesting cobs of colorful popping corn in the fall.

**Grow it**: The key to growing corn in a small space is to grow only one variety. Plants will cross-pollinate among varieties, and the result could be an unhappy surprise. Do grow at least two corn plants of the same variety together to ensure a good crop.

One advantage to growing corn in containers is its shallow root system. The plant doesn't require depth, but it does need good, consistent nutrients. Give your plant lots of nitrogen-based fertilizer such as fish emulsion, provide it with a super-sunny spot, and water regularly. Corn hates waterlogged soil but requires lots of water—finding that balance can be tricky but rewarding.

Sow seeds directly into the pot once the soil has warmed up and all danger of frost is behind you. Corn plants hate to germinate under cold and wet conditions, so hold back from planting too early in climates with cooler spring weather. In colder climates you can always get a head start and grow seeds indoors a few weeks before the last frost date. Transplant them to larger outdoor pots when the temperature heats up.

## Peas (Pisum sativum)

Fresh peas straight off the vine are a delicious sign that spring has begun. Grow quick-producing snow peas or thicker sugar snap varieties. Put a tripod stake in the pot to grow them upward or line up several pots against a trellis to create an edible fence. In smaller spaces try a dwarf variety like 'Tom Thumb', which does not require any staking.

**Grow it:** Peas prefer cool temperatures and are one of the earliest plants to start in spring. Sow a few seeds directly into medium (8-inch diameter) to large containers outside as soon as the ground is thawed. A special legume inoculant powder (purchased at the garden shop) can be applied to the seeds at the time of sowing. Your seeds might grow without it, but an inoculant boosts the yield.

Peas like a sunny spot but will tolerate some shade. Inoculant helps the plant make its own nitrogen but can take a few weeks to get the ball rolling. Give your peas a bit of nitrogen when they're young.

## Potatoes (Solanum tuberosum)

Potatoes might seem like an absurd crop to labor over, but buttery soft new potatoes right out of the garden taste like nothing you've eaten before. And if you grow them yourself, you'll discover cool shapes, flavors, colors, and sizes that you'll never find at the grocery store. My favorite is 'Fingerling', a small, "rustic-flavored" variety that looks like creepy witch's fingers. I also love 'All Blue' and 'Peruvian Purple'—they're brightly colored outside and in.

**Grow it**: Potatoes start from a seed potato, which is nothing fancy, just a baby potato or a piece of a mature one. To make a "seed," cut a large potato into 1½-inch chunks. Each piece must have at least one eye (the gnarly spot where sprouts are formed). Set your seed potatoes in a cool, dark location for a few days to allow the cuts to heal before planting.

Potatoes are easy to grow in the tiniest places. If my grandmother could grow potatoes in a bucket on her balcony, you can, too. The best container for this job is a large bucket or plastic garbage can. The secret is good drainage, so drill some holes in the bottom and the sides of the can. Now, here's the trick: add only 5 to 10 inches of soil to the bottom of the can. Bury your seed potato 3 inches deep and wait for it to grow. Once the vine starts to develop, add more soil, creating a mound around the vine. Continue adding more soil until the can is filled and the vine reaches the top. When your plant begins to turn brown and die it's time to harvest. Turn over the bucket or reach in with your hands and pull out your reward.

## Radishes (Raphanus sativus)

Radishes are an exceptionally easy-to-grow container crop good for the beginner. They're a cool-weather starter with a quick turnaround, so try growing a few crops throughout the growing season.

**Grow it:** Sow radish seeds directly into outdoor containers in the early spring or fall. Don't let plants dry out or get too much direct heat, otherwise they'll bolt and you'll have husky, fiery radishes. In small containers grow compact, round varieties such as 'Easter Egg' or 'Scarlet Globe', and in deep containers try your hand at elongated 'French Breakfast' or 'White Icicle'.

## Peppers (Capsicum annuum)

There are lots of compact, attractive pepper varieties available that do exceptionally well in medium and even smallish containers. Most often these varieties are searing hot peppers such as habanero, aurora, and jalapeño.

If you can't take the heat, grow bell peppers in 18-inch pots. Bells can be just as ornamental as their fiery siblings, with varieties such as 'Sweet Chocolate' or 'Purple Beauty' that mature from plain green to lush brown and dark purple.

**Grow it:** Peppers are perfect for pots since they don't eat much and constricting their roots actually encourages fruit production. They like warm temperatures, so start growing seeds in small pots indoors as much as 10 weeks before the frost-free date. Wait until nighttime temperatures are above 55°F before transplanting them into bigger containers outside. When the first blossoms appear, spray them with a mix of Epsom salts dissolved in water. The magnesium helps fruit set. Provide your plants with lots of sun and warmth (peppers hate the cold) and water steadily throughout the growing season.

# PRETTY DELICIOUS

Traditionally, gardeners section off their space according to plant type. The vegetable garden is practical but hidden, the herb garden is close to the kitchen door, and the flower garden is in the high-traffic area. But why limit yourself to the confines of tradition when you can have it all and eat it, too?

The following plants are exceptionally ornamental and tasty. Better still, they're easy to grow in containers. You'll be super avant-garde for eating your flower patch.

## Sorrel (Rumex)

Hardy perennial. Sorrel is a tart, lemon-flavored leafy herb that grows well in containers. Mine has actually survived cold winters in a large tub and is one of the first plants to pop up from the soil in early spring. The French add it to soups, but I like it chopped into egg salad.

Common sorrel *(Rumex acetosa)* is, well, common, but there are other quite unusual varieties available. Try 'Rhubarb Pie', a whirling dervish of pink, green, cream, gold, and speckles that kind of resembles Christmas on acid. French sorrel *(Rumex scutatus)* is slightly less flamboyant with pretty heart-shaped foliage. 'Silver Shield', a low-growing variety, takes it one step further with a dusting of silver on heart-shaped leaves.

**Grow it:** Sorrel is easy to grow. Give it moist soil and a sunny spot and you'll do just fine. It can tolerate some shade but on the flip side it won't endure a super-hot rooftop. If possible, keep your pot away from extreme heat.

## Strawberries (Fragaria)

Perennial. People are always shocked when I show them my hanging basket of strawberries. Unfortunately, mine have yet to survive the winter in a container. Even so, I grow them every year on my hot deck because a ripe, organic, sun-warmed strawberry is worth every effort.

**Grow it:** Strawberries do just fine in window boxes, pots, or hanging containers. Even better, they don't require huge tubs like most container-grown fruit and can hack the hottest, sunniest spots—perfect for fire escapes and rooftops.

I have grown all types of strawberries on my deck and find hybrids the best for containers because they're built to tolerate some drought and more intense heat. 'Lipstick' is an edible ornamental with pink flowers!

## Swiss Chard (Beta vulgaris)

Hardy perennial. Chard is a leafy green that comes up in early spring and can be harvested leaf by leaf or in bunches throughout the growing season. 'Bright Lights' is a particularly stunning variety that grows into an array of brightly colored stems and leaves. There are also all-red varieties that look great in individual pots.
**Grow it:** Like most greens, chard can take a bit of shade and prefers moist, cool weather. Start seeds or transplants outdoors in early spring and harvest leaves as they grow. You can also cut back the entire plant, leaving a 2-inch stub that will grow into another plant.

## Radicchio (Cichorium intybus)

I love sautéed radicchio on pasta. Some people don't care for radicchio's bitter flavor, but even the most common variety looks ultra-modern minimal in a simple container. Grow a couple in a row or one per small pot. They also look nice as ground cover for potted trees.
**Grow it:** Plants can be grown from seed or purchased in cheap packs of four at the garden center. To harvest, cut the entire head just above the crown with a knife and another plant will grow in its place. You might get one or two harvests this way before the plant gets old and bitter tasting. Just start a fresh batch and keep the harvests coming until the weather is too cold to continue.

## Jerusalem Artichoke (Helianthus tuberosus)

Hardy perennial. Jerusalem artichoke, aka sunchoke, looks like your typical sunflower plant on the outside but produces edible, potato-like tubers under the soil. It is quite a prolific and rather rambunctious plant, so growing in containers can actually be an advantage.
**Grow it:** To grow your own, purchase fresh tubers from a farmer's market or health-food store. Cut each tuber into smaller "seeds" by following the instructions for potatoes found on page 133. Bury one or two "seeds" a few inches below the soil in a medium to large pot (bigger pots equal bigger yields) and set in a sunny, warm spot. By the end of summer you'll have 6- to 10-foot-tall plants! Sunchokes taste best if harvested after a frost, so leave them be until the weather turns nippy. When the time comes, turn the pot over or dig the tubers out.

## Other Edibles to Try

* Amaranth ('Burgundy Splendor')
* Lettuces ('Oakleaf', 'Rouge d'hiver')
* Cress
* Red orach
* Beets ('Bull's Blood')
* Okra ('Red Burgundy')

# POTTED TOMATOES

A basket of colorful, sun-ripened heirloom tomatoes is a gardener's version of sweet, sweet bliss. With a little know-how and determination you can grow your own tomato sauce with the best of them in an environment as inhospitable as a fire escape. Here's how.

## SHE'S GOTTA HAVE IT

The first thing you'll need is sun and lots of it. Tomatoes originate from South America where it is hot—plants require 8 hours of bright light per day for a minimum of 60 days (depending on the variety). This means that you've got to start your tomato seeds early—especially if you live in a cold climate that has short summers. Start your seeds indoors underneath a grow light 6 weeks before the last frost hits your area. Plant them outdoors only after all danger of frost is past.

Tomatoes also need lots of water. Keep this in mind when selecting a location because dragging buckets of water every single day onto a hot deck is no one's idea of a good time.

## TWO TRIBES

Tomatoes come in two types: determinates and indeterminates. You'll know from the plant tag which kind you're getting. Determinates are easy-care plants that tend to stay compact and bushy, making them a good choice for small spaces and hanging baskets. Grow varieties such as 'Tiny Tim' and 'Toy Boy' in midsized containers at least 8 inches deep. Determinates produce cherry-sized tomatoes once per growing season. They're a tasty beginner crop but not the bad boys that make your mouth water.

On the flip side, indeterminates are vining plants that can grow to be 9 feet tall. It is their size that makes them difficult, but not impossible, for container growing. Grow them in the biggest container you can find (garbage bins are great). Staking is not absolutely necessary, but is best for container growing

to ensure maximum use of space and to keep plants off of hot balcony surfaces that can damage fruit. Indeterminate varieties produce all sizes of fruit from cherries to baseballs, depending on the variety. As an added bonus, expect to get a lot of fruit from each plant. Varieties with names like 'Sweet Millions' are no exaggeration!

## STAKING

As soon as you plant your transplants, start staking. Use anything handy, from bamboo poles or scrap wood to metal rods. Plunge the stake into the soil next to your plant and secure the plant to the stake using string or strips of old T-shirt. As the plant grows, loosely tie the vine up the length to continue an upright position. (See All About Staking, page 99).

## PRUNING

Staked plants need pruning early in the growing season to encourage the growth of lots of yummy fruit. Using your thumb and forefinger, pinch off the new stems that pop up between branches (called "suckers"), leaving a few leaves as shade cover for growing tomatoes. Do this at least once a week to stay on top of fast-growing plants.

## GET THE BALANCE RIGHT

Happy tomatoes need a balance of water and fertilizer. How much to water depends on how quickly the water evaporates. Balconies often get intense sun, so you'll need to keep your tomato plants deeply watered by soaking the roots a few times per week. Providing a lot of water at one time is better then a small amount frequently. Small, frequent quantities of water can result in poor root growth, leading to diseases such as blossom-end rot and to skimpy fruit production. To spare your plants nasty fungal diseases, avoid getting the leaves wet. It's best to water the soil directly around the plant rather than spraying the whole plant with a hose.

pinch here

pruning

### Laying on of Hands

Brushing your hands lightly across tomato foliage produces a hormone that promotes stronger, stockier growth.

Begin fertilizing young plants with sea kelp and fish emulsion (according to package directions) once every 2 weeks and continue throughout the growing season. Manure tea (exactly what it sounds like; see page 93) is also a good nutrient source. Be careful not to overdo it. Plants with too much nitrogen will produce lush green leaves and sickly fruit. If this happens, prune like crazy and lay off the fish emulsion. Toss a handful of Epsom salts into the watering can a few times throughout the growing season. The added magnesium prevents blossoms from dropping off prematurely.

## TOMATO 911

Serious diseases and pests are easy to avoid if you take an extra minute to inspect your plants every time you water. Tomatoes are especially susceptible to a disease called tobacco mosaic virus. As a precaution do not smoke cigarettes in close proximity to plants, and if you are a smoker, wash your hands prior to touching or handling fruit and foliage. Plain low-fat milk is an excellent fungicide. Add some to the soil or spray on diseased plants (see page 128).

## GET SOME

Don't settle for the boring usual suspects. Tomatoes are a popular crop for making seeds, and even transplants are easy to come by. Go online to find out about seed trades (try **YouGrowGirl.com**) and greenhouses and organizations that sell all kinds of unusual varieties (see Resources).

If you're planning to grow in a large container, check out heirloom varieties that come in mind-blowing colors and patterns. My personal favorites are 'Black Krim', 'Cherokee Purple', 'Purple Prince', 'Yellow Pear', and 'Orange Banana'.

If small pots are your choice, then specially bred miniature hybrids are the way to go. Remember it's the size of the plant that determines the pot you can use, not the size of the tomato. Many cherry tomato varieties are actually massive indeterminate plants. In really small pots or hanging baskets try varieties such as 'Tiny Tim', 'Toy Boy', or my personal fave and heirloom, 'Sunrise III'. Heirlooms like 'Silver Fir Tree', 'Slava', and 'Black Plum' (pretty dark color with a smoky flavor) will thrive in midsized containers.

# HERBAL TEA GARDEN

After years of being relegated to the world of little old ladies, lace doilies, and the Queen Mum, tea is finally cool again. A cup of tea no longer means a bitter bag of Lipton in a foam cup. Instead it's available at chic tea shops, high-end stores, and yoga centers. The demand for herbal teas in particular has blown up as people have discovered their curative properties. Some herb teas will even provide that morning kick without the crazy caffeine buzz.

Herbal teas are available just about everywhere these days, including your supermarket's beverage aisle. But growing your own means you can have an endless supply of pesticide-free and chemical-free tea fresh off the plant. And most herbs are so easy to grow; with just a bit of know-how and very little money you can assemble your own tea garden in even the worst of conditions. Many tea herbs will tolerate a smallish pot on a cramped but sunny window ledge.

Watch out—some people can experience an allergic reaction to some herbs. Also, certain herbs such as catnip can cause opposite reactions for some people. Before plunging into a full cup of any herbal tea, test a little bit first to ensure everything is copasetic.

Technically speaking, tea is defined as a hot beverage made from steeping the leaves of the *Camellia sinensis* (tea) plant, while any other hot drink concocted from steeping herbs is properly known as a tisane or infusion. There you have it.

# SLEEP AND RELAXATION

## Lavender (Lavandula species)

Perennial. Lavender's relaxing qualities make it an ideal filling for an herbal eye pillow and a wonderfully soothing tea. As a tea it has a soft aromatic flavor that is even yummier with a bit of honey.

Tea is made from lavender flowers, not the leaves and stems. They're best when you pick the flowers just before the buds open.

**Grow it:** While English lavender is a hardy perennial that grow almost effortlessly in a container in all kinds of climates, it is best to move it into the ground or a large, winter-resistant container if you want to grow it into a second year. Its Mediterranean origin means it prefers full sun and well-drained soil and tolerates a little drought, making it an excellent choice for anyone with a hot city fire escape or a penchant for forgetting to water.

## Catnip (Nepeta cataria)

Perennial. Everyone knows about the crazy, narcotic effects catnip can have on cats, but did you know that this kitty dope can have a calming effect on humans? Catnip makes a soothing, minty bedtime tea, but be aware that like cats, some humans will respond to catnip as a stimulant rather than a relaxant. Try a little bit first to be sure that your relaxing cup of tea doesn't unexpectedly act like a late-night cappuccino.

**Grow it:** Catnip grows wild alongside railroad tracks and empty lots and in fallow brown spaces across North America. This stuff practically grows itself, so you can easily grow it from seed in any size pot or even in cracks in the sidewalk. Catnip isn't particularly picky about sun exposure as long as it has rich soil and good airflow around the leaves to avoid the powdery mildew fungal disease it is likely to get. Be aware that if it goes to seed, you'll have a garden full of catnip offspring next season.

## Lemon Balm (Melissa officinalis)

Perennial. Lemon balm is another incredibly prolific tea plant. When brewed as a tea, its leaves have a mild, lemony flavor that is even better than peppermint for relieving stomachaches and headaches. You can use dried leaves for tea, but for a more potent brew, use fresh leaves.

**Grow it:** Under the right conditions lemon balm will spread far and wide across your garden. It likes rich soil with good circulation around the leaves in a cool, partial-shade environment and will burn in full sun. To get the best leaves and the bushiest plant ready for harvest throughout the season, regularly pinch off any flowers or buds as, or before, they form.

## SWEET AND TASTY

### Stevia (Stevia rebaudiana)

Tender Perennial. Long before Cortés showed up, stevia was known in South America as "sweet herb." It makes an excellent and totally healthful herbal sweetener for tea and cooking. This herb is three hundred times sweeter than sugar, so it's way too strong to brew as a straight cup of tea. Instead, add the slightest pinch to your drink to give it a sweet kick. You can use the leaves fresh off the plant or dry them for long-term storage.

**Grow it:** Unfortunately, stevia is a pain in the neck to grow. But with a little know-how and experimentation, you can reap enough in one growing season to keep you and all your friends (and your friends' friends) in sweet tea for the next five years.

Through seasons of trial and error, I have found the key to keeping stevia hearty is a combination of sun (but not too much sun) with rich soil that is kept on the dry side of moist at all times. It absolutely hates wet feet, so be sure your soil drains well and take care after watering container plants to dump any excess water from the tray. Stevia is also very sensitive to cold temperatures. If the pot feels cool to the touch, wrap a blanket or old T-shirt around it (a plant cozy) for added warmth.

### Mint (Mentha species)

Perennial. Notorious for being the most invasive and indestructible of all garden herbs, mint is also the most rewarding and is truly delicious. Amazingly, these days varieties come in every flavor imaginable. By far my favorite variety for tea is chocolate mint, a pretty burgundy plant that smells and tastes like peppermint patties—and it's good for you, too! Try orange or ginger mint for a hint of spice, or to really freak out your friends, serve banana mint tea.

**Grow it:** The great thing about mint is that a small cutting can easily grow into a full-sized plant in no time. You can get yourself an entire garden of assorted mint varieties on the cheap by trading bits and pieces with friends. Generally mint prefers a rich, moist soil in a partially shaded spot. Grow it in pots set into the ground to prevent a hostile mint takeover in your garden.

### Lemon Verbena (Aloysia triphylla)

Tender perennial. Lemon verbena reigns supreme as the tastiest and most refreshingly floral of all the lemon-flavored herbs. Steep the leaves and chill to make a caffeine-free and cheap alternative to those fancy (and pricey!) bottled lemon iced teas.

**Grow it:** In a temperate climate, lemon verbena will grow into a big, woody-stemmed bush. In cooler climates the plant will need to be brought inside to wait out the winter. When inside, keep watering it and don't be alarmed if most or all the leaves drop off. By spring it will bounce back and you can put it back outside. Your plant will flourish in a smallish pot set in full sun.

# BODY BOOSTERS

## Nettle (Urtica dioica)

Perennial. Thriving in wastelands far and wide, nettle is technically defined as a weed. Semantics aside, as a tea it is a nourishing and cleansing tonic that is potently rich in iron and vitamin C—excellent for beating the body blues. It's best to use young leaves harvested in spring. Health foodies love this rather flavorless but incredibly healthful herb.

Making tea from nettle requires a few precautions. It's known as "stinging nettle" for good reason: contact with the tiny hairs that cover the leaves and stems of the plant inflicts major pain. Don't worry, covering up with gloves and long sleeves during harvest will keep you sting-free. Either cooking or drying will disarm the stinging bristles. But do one or both before consuming; raw leaves can cause kidney damage—not that anyone would be able to get past even a nibble of raw nettle! To make a tea, add a few teaspoons of dried leaves to a cup of boiling water. Toss in a sprig of mint to give this healthy tea some flavor.

**Grow it:** Nettle grows best in moist, rich soil with lots of sun. It is easily propagated from seeds or cuttings. But it's such a common weed, growing it on purpose may not be necessary!

## Rose Hips (Rosa species)

Perennial. You may have heard of grandma's finicky, fussy tea roses and have opted not to bother. It turns out that there are rose varieties that make a yummy and healthful tea and are a breeze to grow!

Rose petals have a delicate, floral taste used to flavor black tea (called China rose tea). But it's the hips (immature seedpods) that rock the delicious fruity flavor and incredibly high vitamin C content. One cup of rose hip tea is equivalent to the cold-fighting power of more than one hundred oranges! Rose hips develop on the plant after the flower has done its thing. Generally the best time to harvest the hips is right after the first frost. Overripe hips are sweeter but lack vitamin potency, so be sure to pick hips that are on the redder side of orange. Rose hips can be chopped fresh and steeped for several minutes or dried and stored for future use (see page 157 for tips on drying herbs).

**Grow it:** Wild varieties such as members of the rugosa species are the most resistant to disease and the easiest to grow. They require very little maintenance and tolerate all kinds of growing conditions. Keep in mind that they prefer well-drained soil and good air circulation around the leaves. Of course the hips of any rose species will do, but the easygoing nature of the wild species makes them the best choice for gardeners with other things to do besides fuss over their roses.

## Dill (Anethum graveolens)

Annual. It turns out that dill, as in the dill in dill pickles, packs a healthy punch. Dill tea is an excellent tonic for quietly calming an upset stomach, stimulating a fussy appetite, or freshening bad breath. The leaves are best picked from young plants, but seeds also make good-tasting, healthful tea.

**Grow it:** It's easy to grow dill from seed. Just throw the seeds onto the garden bed or into a pot in the spring. Dill plants aren't happy about being moved around, so direct sowing is the way to go. Like most herbs, it prefers a well-drained soil and lots of sun.

## A FRESH INFUSION

Theoretically, all it takes to make a cup of tea from fresh herbs is hot water, the herbs, and a cup. Then why do I have a cupboard full of tea-making gear? No one wants twigs and leaves interfering with their sipping pleasure, and different equipment works for different circumstances. Tea balls, special slotted teaspoons, and miniature bamboo tea baskets are all good cheap options to help steep your tea. A plunger-style coffee brewer works well with herbs that don't turn bitter quickly. Some traditional teapots supply a built-in straining device. You can buy empty tea bags from specialty stores or try making your own reusable cotton bags (see instructions page 148). All of these are great options, but I personally prefer some ritual around making my cup of tea. Try these steps to prepare a fancy, finicky cup of tea:

**1.** Bring a pot of cool distilled or bottled water to a boil. Let it sit for a few minutes to cool down slightly. Boiled water is too strong and can evaporate the active oils in the herb, ruining medicinal value and flavor.

**2.** While waiting for the water to boil, go out to your garden and clip some fresh herbs into a cloth tea bag. Use 2 teaspoons of fresh herbs for each cup of tea. If using dried herbs, use 1 teaspoon per cup. For information on drying and storing herbs, see page 157.

**3.** Splash some hot water into your cup or pot, slosh around to prewarm it, then dump the water.

**4.** Set the tea bag into the cup or pot and pour hot water over the herbs. When using a cup, brew with a saucer or lid on top to prevent the good stuff from evaporating.

**5.** Steep to taste. Steeping can take anywhere from 5 to 15 minutes, depending on the herb.

**6.** Sweeten to taste or drink as is. Honey is the popular tea sweetener, but a mild maple syrup is also delicious. Some sweet herbs such as stevia (see page 144) or even mint can be added to heighten the intensity of another herb.

## SUN-POWERED TEA

You can make tea without leaving your garden! Native Americans (and hippies) have long practiced brewing tea using the heat of the sun instead of a kettle. The theory is that boiling water introduces bitter oils into the drink while removing the better flavors of the herb, but setting it in the sun gives you all the goodness and none of the bitterness.

On a sunny summer afternoon, try making your own sun tea using a few herb leaves (seeds and roots require much hotter water) and a clean glass mason jar. Snip a few fresh leaves from your favorite herb and place in the jar. Fill the jar with water, attach the lid, and place in hot sun for 3 to 6 hours. The sun will actually warm up the jar and start a slow, gentle brewing process. Too much time is not a good thing—some herbs release tannic acid after a few days. Also, sun tea should be drunk or refrigerated within 8 hours of brewing to avoid problems with bacteria. If you want a stronger tea in a shorter time span, use more herbs. Once brewed, pour through a strainer to remove any herb bits and enjoy. Try adding some ice for iced sun tea!

# EASY-SEW TEA BAGS

Lots of fancy tea dealers sell their tea in simple fabric bags, and some even sell empty bags for brewing. But why spend when, with minimal sewing skill and a few bucks, you can make a ton of your own reusable tea bags? Friends will swoon when they get a homemade tea bag filled with homegrown herbs for their birthday!

**1.** Fold down ½ inch of fabric from the top and press with a hot iron. This creates a pocket for the drawstrings.

**2.** Open the fold and lay one string flat across from end to end. Fold back down and straight stitch a ¼-inch seam across, being sure to avoid sewing on top of the string. Repeat steps 1 and 2 on the opposite side.

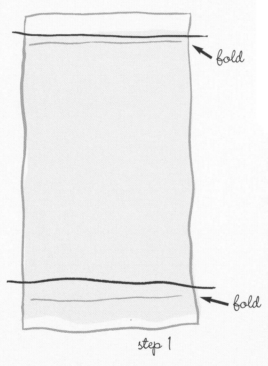

fold

fold

step 1

## You Will Need

* One 3½-by-9-inch rectangle of cheap cotton muslin (unbleached is best)
* An iron
* Two 6-inch pieces of thin cotton string
* Matching thread
* Sewing machine (or needle)
* Needle with a large eye (big enough to fit the string)

**3.** Fold the bag in half, matching the two finished edges. Sew a ¼-inch seam along the sides of the bag, stopping at the drawstring pockets.

**4.** Tie the strings together into a knot at each end. Turn the bag right side out and pull the strings from one end to close.

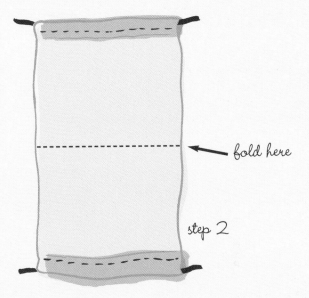

fold here

step 2

step 3

*Voilà, you have your own reusable gourmet tea bag ready for fresh or dried herbs. Repeat as necessary to make tea bags for all of your friends.*

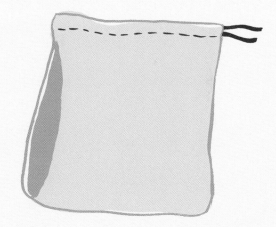

finished tea bag

# BOUNTY

The end of the gardening season is such a bittersweet time. Weekend mornings spent in the garden with a glass of tea and a good book may be about to come to an end, but on the flip side exciting things are happening all around. This is the time of year when most of your favorite veggies reach their peak for picking—tomatoes by the bowl full, fresh potatoes and corn, and more peppers than you can shake a stick at. Now's your opportunity to harvest the fruits of your labor and enjoy the rewards. My favorite harvest activity is sitting outside in a comfy chair on a sunny day picking leaves off stacks of smellerific basil stems. I puff my chest with pride, fantasizing about all the delicious meals I will enjoy in the near future and how I will take over the world with my awesome basil-growing prowess. Other rewarding, late-season activities are harvesting seeds for next year's crop and collecting extra seeds to give as gifts or to trade with gardening buddies.

This chapter gives you tips, info, and ideas to guide you through how to harvest the goods to get the most mileage from your herb, flower, or other edible crops. It also gives you unique and useful preparation, preservation, and storage ideas suited to the gardener who's got more garden than space.

This chapter shows you how to make and grow your own organic beauty and bath products better than the stuff you'd pay mucho dinero for in specialty stores, and transform leftover green tomatoes into tasty chutney. There are so many cool ways to use up your garden booty, the hard part is really a matter of deciding what to try first!

# COLLECTING THE BOOTY

When and how to harvest the good stuff depends on what you've got. The general rule is pick it fresh and pick it small. Veggies and fruit from your garden are better than almost anything else in life, but if left to mature too long they taste bland or have a woody texture. Salad from the garden can be heavenly, but overgrown lettuce greens are bitter and sappy like glue.

The life cycle of most plants follows the standard high school biology script: plant develops leaves and stems, flowers appear, flowers are pollinated, fruit develops, and finally seeds develop and mature. Some plants, known as annuals, will die after they've achieved their final goal of producing seeds. Perennial plants remain alive even after they've popped out their seeds, although their top growth may die back. Most garden vegetables and some herbs are annuals that call it quits once they've developed fruit. If it is fruit that you're after (tomatoes and even zucchinis fall into this category), harvesting as they develop encourages the plant to produce more fruit because it hasn't yet achieved its goal.

The same goes for leafy plants. You can beat your plant at its own game by picking back the leaves as the plant grows. This will prevent the onset of flowers and seeds that would normally bring the plant to the end of its growing cycle and give you a larger harvest over the season.

## HERBS

Leafy herbs like basil, chervil, or stevia grow stockier, bushier, and yield more when you do mini-harvests throughout the growing season. Trim back the top few inches (leaves and stems included) with scissors, or pick off a few leaves to use for dinner. If it's flowers you're after, cut them off when

they're at their prime, just after the buds begin to open and well before seeds develop. It pays to be an early bird—harvest parts in the morning when tasty aromatic oils are at their peak. (See page 155 for tips on preserving your extra herbs).

Wait until the end of the plant's growing season to harvest a large quantity of leaves from annual herbs like basil for pesto or long-term storage. In cold climates lift annuals straight out of the ground (since they won't come back next year), then dry the entire plant for long-term storage. Perennials such as sage or oregano can be pruned right back in preparation for winter. Leave the rest of the plant in the ground so you'll have a new crop next year.

## LEAFY GREENS

Get extra mileage out of lettuce crops like arugula, spinach, mizuna, and other leafy greens by harvesting individual outer leaves once the plant is 5 inches tall or so. If you keep harvesting a few leaves at a time, lettuce will keep growing and giving you salad fixin's all season long. Alternately, wait until the plant has developed a full head and lop it off with a sharp knife or a pair of scissors an inch or so above the base. The plant will regenerate into a whole new head in a few weeks. One head of lettuce can be harvested this way two or three times before it turns bitter. Once it's maxed out, dig up the root and throw it in the compost bin. Greens are fast-growing crops, so replace finished plants with new seeds and you'll have a continuous supply well into fall or straight through the year in warm climates.

# FRUITS AND VEGETABLES

It is easy to tell when most fruits and vegetables are ripe for the picking by the way they look or feel—deepening color or becoming soft and squishy are sure signs of ripeness. Crops that grow belowground can be a bit trickier. The condition of the leaves and stems is generally a good gauge of what is going on below the surface. Mature potatoes are ready for digging when the leaves have died back. Pull up onions when the tops fall over. Of course this method isn't foolproof. Carrot leaves don't die back, but generally the carrot root will push its way through the soil surface when it's ready.

Every plant has a different schedule and a peak picking time. Most veggies should be picked just before the first frost, but a few exceptions like parsnip achieve perfection after a cold snap. In warmer climates you'll have to check for ripeness rather than relying on the weather to remind you to bring the crops in. Most crops will not ripen off the plant, so be sure it's ready before jumping the gun. If you're unsure what the crop looks like when ripe, visit a produce market to get a look or consult a vegetable and fruit gardening book (see Resources).

# HARVEST TIPS

✳ **Bigger Is Not Better**—Don't wait for vegetables to grow into monster-sized versions of the ones you see in stores unless they are specially bred to be large. An oversize zucchini sure seems like a major score, but it won't have the tender, fresh flavor of a regular-sized zucchini. Veggies that are left on the vine too long will eventually grow tasteless and tough.

✳ **More, More, More**—Increase your harvest of vegetables such as cucumber, beans, and peas by picking them faster. These plants will stop producing altogether if you leave them too long on the vine. Vegetable plants are on a mission to reproduce. Once they've done their thing, it's game over. A regular harvest tricks the plant into trying for a second and third inning.

✳ **Fresh Food Now**—Pick vegetables and fruit just before you're going to eat them. If you plan to store them over the long term, this doesn't apply. But most crops taste best fresh off the vine and lose their flavor if left to hang around on the counter or in the fridge for too long.

## How to Ripen Green Tomatoes

You'll have harvested most of your tomatoes before fall, but if you live in a climate that freezes, those remaining green stragglers need to be picked before the first frost. To ripen a bounty of end-of-season green tomatoes, place them individually in paper bags or wrap them in pieces of newspaper to prevent rot. Warmth rather than light is essential to fast ripening, so keep them in a cozy spot. Contrary to popular belief, a sunny window ledge is not necessary. On top of the fridge works amazingly!

If you've got space to spare, lift the entire tomato plant from the ground—roots, green fruit, and all—and hang upside down in a garage or shed. It's an easy way to guarantee that the leftover fruit will get red and delicious in a matter of days.

When all else fails, turn the stubborn, unripe few into fried green tomatoes or green tomato chutney. Yum.

# GREEN TOMATO CHUTNEY

This chutney recipe is "quick and dirty"—intended to be used up rather than canned for long-term storage. It can be kept in the fridge for about a week. Chutney tastes good as a condiment served with just about anything. I like it on a piece of toast.

## You Will Need

* 1 pound diced green tomatoes (about 4 to 6 medium)
* 2 tablespoons finely chopped shallots
* 1 medium apple, chopped (about 1 cup)
* ½ cup raisins
* ¼ cup apple cider vinegar
* 1 finely minced clove of garlic
* 1 teaspoon finely minced fresh ginger
* ⅛ teaspoon ground cayenne pepper
* 2 tablespoons water
* Pinch of salt

**1.** Place all ingredients in a medium saucepan. Cook on high heat, stirring until the mixture comes to a boil.

**2.** Reduce to medium heat and simmer for 15 to 20 minutes until the mixture has thickened and some of the liquid has evaporated. Stir regularly.

**3.** Remove from the heat and let the chutney cool before serving.

Makes 2 cups.

## EAT LESS DIRT: WASHING HERBS AND PRODUCE

If you're growing organic, heavy washing is probably an unnecessary hassle. Most organic veggies do fine with a quick rinse. Give root vegetables a rinse and a scrub with a loofah sponge or a produce brush before cooking or preparing for a meal. Washing produce too far ahead of time can actually shorten its storage life by removing the natural layer that prevents rot.

For extra-gritty or nonorganic veggies, soak them in a bowl of water spiked with a few drops of chemical-free dish detergent. Or, if you're concerned about nonorganic manure on produce, add a few drops of grapefruit seed extract concentrate (aka Citiricidal, a natural antimicrobial) to wash water.

# UNTIL TOMORROW

It is possible with even a small garden to produce an abundance of at least one crop that's worth saving for the future. Herbs and flowers are the most likely candidates in a small space, with tomatoes following closely behind. Every year I grow enough basil to support my addiction well through to the next harvest. Complicated preservation methods such as canning can be sweaty, intense work, but there are a few easy methods for lazy folk, too.

## FREEZING

Freezing is a simple and space efficient method, perfect for the apartment dweller, since bags of frozen goods can be crammed into the back of the freezer. Rental apartment freezers are sadly undependable, but I've managed to keep my precious herb supply fresh over the years despite fluctuating freezer temperatures.

### To Fresh-Freeze Herbs

Most herbs do well in the freezer, but don't expect fresh leaves to come out the way they went in. Freezing turns leaves mushy but keeps the flavor intact. Use frozen herbs for cooking or tea and the mushiness won't matter. Try freezing basil, oregano, sage, chives, tarragon, lemongrass, mint, thyme, summer savory, and dill.

**1.** Pluck the best leaves and flowers from stems.

**2.** Rinse herbs in a colander and spin dry using a salad spinner. If you don't have one, pat dry with a clean towel. Leaves do not need to be bone dry.

**3.** Store your stash in small resealable plastic bags or seal it up using a handy vacuum-seal device. For thawing convenience, package your herbs in small single-meal quantities. Use up your thawed herbs quickly—they'll go bad even quicker than fresh herbs.

### Freezing Veggies and Fruit

Freezing is best for hearty veggies, including peppers, beans, peas, winter squash, and berries. Some soft veggies such as zucchini turn into an unappetizing, slimy mess after a stint in the freezer. If you're going to freeze these veggies, use them in soups rather than stir-fries.

**1.** Wash and chop larger vegetables into manageable chunks.

**2.** Most vegetables do better in the freezer after a short stint in boiling water (called blanching). Blanching prevents the loss of color, texture, and nutritional value. To blanch, gently drop your chopped veggies into a pot of boiling water. After a minute, when their color has brightened, pull the veggies out with a slotted spoon or pour the water and veggies into a colander to strain. Immediately pop the veggies into icy water to stop the cooking.

**3.** Drain veggies from the icy water and let them dry before packaging them up.

**4.** Store in meal-sized portions in freezer bags. Before sealing the bags, squeeze out as much air as possible.

### Easy Freeze

Sweet peppers do not require blanching before freezing. Simply chop them up and pop them in a freezer bag. You'll have fresh, homegrown peppers all winter long.

## OILY HERB PASTE

Best for leafy herbs such as basil, oregano, and thyme. This method produces a pestolike paste rather than flavored oil. It basically *is* pesto, minus the garlic, nuts, and cheese. This is my favorite way to fresh-store my much-loved basil reserves. The oil keeps the basil super fresh and ready for use in sauces, soups, and as a spread.

## You Will Need

* 3 cups fresh herb leaves
* ½ cup oil (olive or other)
* Pinch of salt

**1.** Thoroughly wash and dry herb leaves and flowers in a salad spinner.

**2.** Place clean herbs in a food processor or blender with the oil and salt. Pulse until the leaves are chopped to a paste.

**3.** Spoon the paste into small resealable plastic bags. Push all the air out of the bags and freeze.

**4.** Thawed herb paste can be stored in the fridge for two weeks.

Makes approximately 1 cup paste.

## DRYING

Drying is an outstanding way to keep herbs over the long term. While drying enhances the flavor of some herbs, it morphs the flavor of others into something peculiar. As an example, I'm horrified by dried sweet basil but love dried 'Dark Opal' basil sprinkled on pizza. Lemon basil is also particularly tasty dried, as are lemon verbena, lemon balm, mint, and thyme.

You can also dry a surprising number of veggies for long-term storage. Tie small hot peppers, onions, and garlic into bundles with string and hang in a well-ventilated area until they're bone dry.

## HOW TO DRY HERBS

**1.** Choose a sunny day to harvest your plants when the leaves aren't wet from rain or watering. Cut the stems with a sharp pair of pruners.

**2.** Don't wash herbs before drying them—washed herbs dry into a brown, unsightly mess and sometimes go moldy. Shake the dirt off instead. If you must wash, thoroughly pat dry with a towel before hanging.

**3.** Bind the stems together in small bunches with an elastic band.

**4.** Tie an 8-inch piece of string around each bundle. You're likely to forget which is which, so mark each bundle with a tag.

**5.** Hang herb bundles in a dry, well-ventilated area out of direct light. I hang mine under the gazebo tent on my deck.

**6.** In about 2 weeks, depending on humidity, the herbs will be dry and ready for long-term storage.

If you don't have a place to dry herbs, an oven set at the lowest temperature will do the job. Spread herbs (with stems intact) on a tray. Open the oven door a crack and stand watch, staying at the ready. Most herbs should be bone dry in a few minutes.

If you have one, a food dehydrating machine is another choice option for drying any and all herbs. Follow manufacturer's instructions.

## STORING DRIED HERBS

Dried herbs can be stored loosely in glass jars. You can still find pretty old jars at thrift stores or new mason jars at hardware and home stores. Small resealable plastic bags and paper bags aren't quite as classy but certainly are practical and save space. For the long term, place dried herbs in freezer bags and into the freezer. To make compact packages, strip leaves from stems and whiz the leaves up in an electric coffee mill or blender before storing.

*Thrifty Drying*

Construct a makeshift drying rack from a wire coat hanger slung over a door frame. Choose an out-of-the-way place light on foot traffic. Bind bundles of herbs with string and tie them to the bottom bar.

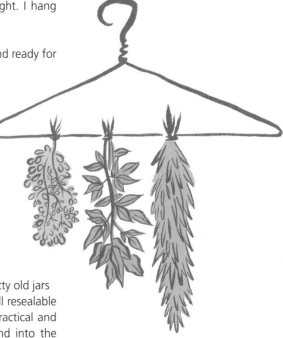

# BATH & BEAUTY PLANTS

Herbs were used in beauty products long before cosmetic companies started manufacturing souped-up versions using ingredients with long, unpronounceable names. Lately consumers have wised up and figured out that some of those ancient traditions actually did the trick. And now companies are starting to capitalize on the growing trend toward products with a natural and homemade vibe by charging double! So why not grow your own herbs, make your own cosmetics, and save a few bucks? Doing it yourself is easy, fun, and creative, and you can do your own quality control.

Start by growing these herbs, then use them as ingredients in the body food recipes that follow. Steps for growing other useful bath and body herbs, including mint, lavender, and lemon verbena, are on pages 143–145.

## Herbal Beauty Guide

**Refreshing**—Mint, lemongrass, eucalyptus, rosemary, basil
**Relaxing**—Chamomile, lavender, lemon balm, catnip
**Healing**—Calendula, comfrey, aloe, rose

## Aloe Vera (Aloe vera)

Tender perennial. Aloes are a lovely, sculptural group of succulents native to South Africa. Aloe vera (aka *Aloe barbadensis*) is best known for its healing properties and use as a beauty aid. Cut a portion from a fresh leaf and rub the soothing gel on cuts and sunburns, or use on dry skin as a moisturizer. The leaf portion remaining on the plant will actually heal itself over in a few days. I keep a potted plant handy as an instant, living first-aid kit.

**Grow it:** In tropical or frost-free locations, aloe can grow into a massive plant outdoors. The rest of us can enjoy smaller plants grown in pots. Take it outside during the summer and remember to bring it back indoors before the first frost.

Aloes prefer filtered sun and may actually burn if the heat is too direct. Water potted plants every week during the growing season, but allow the soil to dry a bit between watering. During the winter dormant period your plant won't grow much, so water it only every two weeks or so. Excess water will cause it to rot!

## Calendula (Calendula officinalis)

Annual. Also known as pot marigold, but don't let the name fool ya—calendula looks more like an orange daisy than it does a typical marigold. The bright flowers have a myriad of uses. Most often you'll find it in beauty products to sooth skin irritations, but it can also be made into natural cosmetics and fabric dye. It's also

good to eat—a few petals thrown in a pot of rice make a poor gal's saffron. Fresh young leaves or petals are tasty (and colorful) in a salad.

Make your own soothing calendula skin oil following the directions for an herbal infusion (see Gardener's Healing Hand Salve, page 162).

**Grow it:** Although the "pot" in pot marigold refers to the cooking kind, this bright and cheery herb does well in containers. Like most herbs it prefers well-drained, rich soil. Pick flowers before they mature to keep them coming, but leave a few on at the end of the season to allow the plant to self-seed and produce a new crop in the spring.

## Comfrey (Symphytum species)

Hardy perennial. Comfrey is another excellent healing and soothing herb useful for rejuvenating and healing skin. It's an important ingredient in skin creams.

This plant is incredibly invasive with a long taproot that is difficult to remove once it has established itself. Be sure to choose an out-of-the-way place in the garden where it won't overpower other plants. Luckily, what you don't use for beauty products can be made into a quality fertilizer—those long roots pull nutrients up from deep in the soil! (See Rank Tea, page 93).

**Grow it:** A crop of comfrey will fare well in moist soil in a partially shady spot. It is a huge plant that will survive only in very large containers—garbage pails work well. Despite its healing properties, comfrey leaves are covered with bristly hairs that scratch. If you're sensitive to bristly foliage like I am, wear gloves and arm protection before pruning or harvesting the plant.

## Rosemary (Rosemarinus officinalis)

Tender perennial. Fragrant rosemary leaves are delicious on roasted potatoes and make a nourishing herb for your body. The plant is best known as a memory and brain percolator. Drink a cup of rosemary tea to cure a nasty headache. Pour some over your head to stimulate the scalp while you're at it, or sprinkle some in the bath to sooth the nerves and perk up your entire body.

**Grow it:** Rosemary does well in warm, sunny locations—the result of its Mediterranean heritage. In warm or temperate climates it can actually grow into large, fragrant hedges. Opt for smaller potted plants if you're in a cool climate, and be sure to bring it indoors for the winter. Generally, rosemary is an herb best left to its own devices. Give it occasional attention, but I find the more it is doted on, the less it grows.

### Trim That Bush

In Old England, a rosemary bush flourishing in the garden was indication that a strong matriarch ruled the home. This belief intensified the battle of the sexes, causing men to secretly destroy rosemary bushes to hide the evidence.

# BODY FOOD

Herbs and flowers are the foundation ingredient in many popular body-care products. You can actually make your own skin and bath treats—using ingredients from your own garden!

## PEPPERMINT FOOT SCRUB

This refreshing scrub revives tired, dry feet and is a good use for overgrown mint crops.

**1.** Coarsely chop mint leaves in a blender or food processor. Add water as needed to aid the process.

**2.** In a bowl, combine the chopped mint, sea salt, and oil. Your mix should be thick and pasty.

**3.** Rub on feet and scrub lightly. Rinse.

**4.** Apply as often as your tired dogs need it.

Makes 1 cup of foot scrub.

*Peppermint Foot Scrub can be stored in a jar and refrigerated for a few days.*

### You Will Need

* 1 cup mint
* ½ cup water
* 1½ cups sea salt
* ½ teaspoon sweet almond oil or olive oil

# HERBAL HAIR RINSE

Wash these herbal concoctions through your hair as a final rinse. They promote shine and enhance natural hair color. You can use fresh or dried herbs, but double the quantity when using fresh herbs.

Brunettes should use rosemary and sage, while blondes should use chamomile and calendula.

*Use the rinse right away or keep it in the fridge for up to a week.*

**1.** Over low heat, simmer all ingredients in a saucepan for 30 minutes.

**2.** Set aside to cool.

**3.** Strain the liquid into a glass mason jar or bottle.

Makes 1 cup of hair rinse.

## You Will Need

* ½ cup dried or 1 cup fresh herb leaves and/or flowers
* 5 cups water
* 1 tablespoon cider vinegar
* Saucepan
* Mason jar or bottle

# GARDENER'S HEALING HAND SALVE

Gardeners can get dry, cracked skin from soil sucking the moisture from their hands as they dig. Avoid this beauty hazard by rubbing this salve into your skin after gardening to prevent or heal chapped, dry skin.

**1.** Your first job is to make an herbal infusion. Steep the calendula and lavender flowers in oil and gently warm in a double boiler over low heat for 1 to 3 hours. DO NOT allow the oil to boil.

**2.** Using a slotted spoon or a sieve, strain the flower particles from the oil and discard.

**3.** Return the oil to the double boiler and add the cocoa butter and beeswax. Melt over low heat.

**4.** Once melted, remove from the heat.

**5.** Pop 2 vitamin E capsules with a pin, squeeze, and add the oil to the mix. Essential oil may be added at this point if you like a stronger-scented balm.

**6.** Stir with a chopstick until the ingredients are well blended.

**7.** Pour into a metal tin or jar for keeping. In a few minutes, the mix will harden into a salve that can be rubbed into dry skin.

Makes approximately 4 to 6 ounces of Healing Hand Salve.

*Gardener's Healing Hand Salve lasts for 3 to 6 months. Create a cool label or use a nice jar and it makes a great gift for fellow gardeners.*

## You Will Need

* 2 tablespoons dried calendula flowers
* 2 tablespoons dried lavender flowers
* 4 tablespoons sweet almond oil or olive oil
* Double boiler (or a wide-mouth mason jar set in a small saucepan of water)
* Slotted spoon or sieve
* 1½ tablespoons cocoa butter*
* 2½ tablespoons grated beeswax*
* 2 capsules vitamin E
* 10 drops lavender essential oil (optional)
* Chopsticks for stirring
* 1 metal tin or small wide-mouth jar (to hold approximately 4 ounces)

* Can usually be purchased at your local health food store.

# LOOFAH BATH SCRUB

Get this: your shower sponge is a vegetable. A loofah sponge may look like some kind of hi-tech plastic, but it's 100 percent natural and you can grow your own.

The loofah is an annual climbing vine related to cucumbers that produces extremely fibrous gourds. Once cleaned and dried, these gourds can be used as scrubbers to wash your dishes, scrub veggies, or slough dead skin cells from your body (not all at once!). They can be washed for continued use and stored indefinitely, so one crop may be enough to keep you and all your friends in sponges for the next few years.

## GROW IT

Sponge loofahs require a growing season of at least 110 days. In warm climates, plant your seeds directly into the soil. But in colder climates with short growing seasons you'll need to start your seeds indoors 3 weeks prior to the final frost-free date to ensure ample ripening time.

Loofahs require moist soil and lots of sun to produce plump, good-sized sponges, so be certain to water regularly and deeply. Choose a sunny location for planting and add a blanket of mulch to conserve moisture.

You can try growing your loofah plant in a container, but you'll need to do some extra planning. Do not underestimate the massive vine that tiny seedling will quickly become! Get the biggest pot you can find. A medium or large plastic garbage can or five gallon bucket with drainage holes drilled in the bottom will do the job. Water, water, water! Containers placed on hot decks and rooftops lose water quickly. Don't let the soil dry out for any stretch of time.

### Speedy Seed Starting

Gourds can be slow germinators. You can speed up the process by lightly scraping the seed coating with sandpaper (called scarifying), then give the seeds a good soak overnight in room-temperature water and plant the following day.

As your plant matures, it will look like a long, leafy string of oversized cucumbers. You're going to need some support to keep those hefty loofahs off the ground, or they will rot. Shortly after planting, set a sturdy tripod (aka teepee) staking system or trellis next to your plant as support. Alternatively, plant your seedlings along a fence to create a living wall of loofah (see page 99 for staking tips).

## HARVESTING

Fresh, green gourds can be harvested young and cooked like squash. By late summer or early fall, gourds will begin to lose weight and change color. This is a sign that they are beginning to mature into sponges. Cut your loofahs from the vine only after they are dry, have turned brown or yellow, and make a rattling sound when shaken. Store them in a dry location until you are ready to clean them.

## CLEANING

**1.** Using a sharp knife, cut the ends off each loofah and shake all the seeds out. Seeds can be dried and stored for next year's crop (see Seed Harvest, page 166).

**2.** Submerge the dried gourd in water for a few minutes until it has softened enough that the skin begins to peel up.

**3.** Peel off the skin and remove the residual pulp from inside the cavity by scooping it out with a spoon.

**4.** Now do a second soak in a 3:1 mix of water and hydrogen peroxide until the sponge looks clean.

**5.** Rinse out all the hydrogen peroxide and place the sponge on a rack in the sun to dry.

**6.** Tie a piece of butcher's twine or natural jute to one end for handy hanging in the shower.

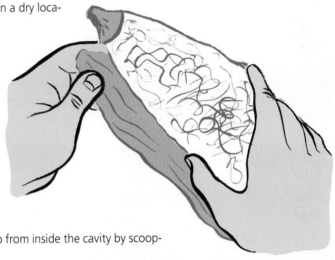

TIP

Loofahs will cross-pollinate with other gourd types, producing unpredictable results. If you are planning to grow other gourd varieties, keep your plants on opposite ends of the garden.

# SEED HARVEST

Kick that go-nowhere dependency on the seed pusher! Some simple grade-school botany and this easy-to-follow guide will lead you on the path to a steady supply of seeds that you can save or trade to grow your plant collection for free. Stick it to the man by harvesting your own.

## SMACKDOWN: OPEN POLLINATED VS. HYBRIDS

Before saving seeds from a particular plant, you will need to know whether it is a hybrid or open pollinated (aka OP). Hybrids are plants that have been purpose-fully bred using two different species of the same plant to produce specific, desirable traits. The tomatoes you buy in the supermarket are a good example of this. These varieties have been bred for tough skins necessary to endure transportation across the country, but they often lack on the taste side. This is one reason why you may not want to save seeds from store-bought produce.

Seeds packaged for the home gardener by seed companies may also be hybridized. These plants are usually bred to be larger than life, beautiful, and flamboyant—the drag queens of the garden. The problem with hybrids is that they are often sterile. Or, if they do produce viable seed, the traits are not carried over to the next generation. Growing these seeds is a gamble. You never know what you'll get.

On the other hand, open-pollinated plants are pollinated (by humans or nature) by the same species of plant. Heirlooms—older plant varieties that have remained unchanged for several generations—fall into this category. Checking the seed packet or grower's catalog is one way to determine the status of your seed. Packets are marked F1 to indicate hybrids and OP to indicate open pollinated.

## SEED HARVEST HOW-TO

If this is your first attempt at seed saving, get your feet wet slowly with plants that flawlessly produce seeds without intervention. Annuals such as cosmos, pansies, snapdragons, and marigolds are a good start. Collect seeds from healthy, vibrant plants. Diseased plants will only pass their problems on.

Under typical circumstances, snipping flower heads off after they are spent (deadheading) encourages annuals to continue making flowers like it's 1999. To get seed, all you have to do is stop the party and let the plant shift its energy into the next stage—making babies. Before long, seedpods will grow in place of the spent flowers. Don't remove the seed head right away; leave it to ripen on the plant. Seeds are generally ready when the pod turns brown, dries out, or cracks open. Once this happens, cut the stem or seedpods off the plant.

*Brown Bag It*

Cover plants that spill their seed easily (snapdragons, pansies, catnip, poppies) with lunch-sized paper bags and tie them on using an elastic band or string. This contraption will catch the seeds as they fall. When the stem has dried and the seeds are popping into the bag, cut the stem low on the plant and shake the seedpods inside the bag to dislodge them.

If the seed heads are not fully ripe when removed, either hang the stems (with seedpods attached) or lay them flat to dry on a newspaper or paper towel away from direct sunlight. Make sure your seeds are completely dry before removing them from the pods. If you package them too early they will go moldy in storage. It's easier to dry the whole seed head than a bunch of loose seeds.

When the pod is dry, break it open and pull the seeds from the casing. Separate the tiny seeds from seed-casing debris through a fine mesh strainer or screen.

## HARVESTING VEGETABLE SEEDS

You can collect most vegetable seeds without much fuss. Choose healthy produce that is ripe and at its peak, before rot and decay have set in. Cut or scoop out the seeds from inside the plant and wash them under water to remove pulp. Leave cleaned seeds to dry on pads of newspaper or a mesh screen.

There's always an exception, and this time it's beans—leave bean pods on the vine until they dry, then simply remove the seeds and package them.

## FERMENTING TOMATO SEEDS

If you've ever cut open a tomato you've seen that the seeds are coated by a slimy, gelatinous layer. This substance contains chemicals that prevent the seeds from germinating inside the tomato (called germination inhibiter). Plants are smart! Fermenting your seeds is an easy (and smelly) process that naturally destroys that protective layer so seeds can be packaged for storage. Fermentation also destroys some pathogens, preventing the spread of disease from last year's mishaps.

**1.** Cut a tomato in half and scoop or squish the seeds and pulp into a clean plastic yogurt container. Lids aren't required.

**2.** Label each container with the variety name and place in a warm spot away from direct sunlight. Find somewhere out of the way. This is going to stink!

**3.** Stir each container a couple of times per day. After a few days you should find a layer of white mold resembling a science experiment gone wrong or the remains of dinner from two weeks ago. Nasty! Don't leave this too long or your seeds will start to germinate.

**4.** During the fermentation process the good seeds will sink to the bottom and everything else will stay on top with the moldy layer. To separate, pour off the moldy layer and liquid. Use a spoon to scoop it off if you're having trouble. Be careful not to let the good seeds escape.

*All that mold means it's ready!*

*Fill 'er up with fresh water.*

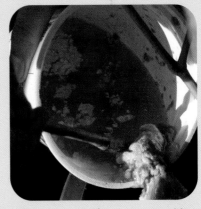

*Scoop out the nasty stuff that floats on top.*

**5.** Fill the container with water, stir it all up, and slowly pour out the water, letting all the bad seeds dump out with the water.

**6.** Repeat step 5 a few times until most of the bad seeds and debris have been washed away.

**7.** Dump the remaining good seeds into a strainer and give them a good rinse.

**8.** Spread the good seeds on a pad of newspaper or paper coffee filters. Set them out to dry for a few days. Don't forget to label them!

**9.** Package dried seeds in paper envelopes.

## STORING SEEDS

Paper or plastic? The best way to store seeds is to package them in paper envelopes or bags instead of plastic since seeds will turn moldy or prematurely germinate in humid conditions. A cool, dark, and dry cupboard with a consistent temperature is an ideal spot for storage. You can store oversized seeds (beans) or large batches of small seeds in glass mason jars. Label your packets and containers with the name and date of harvest—you think you'll remember but I guarantee you won't. If you're planning to give seeds to friends as gifts, go that extra mile and include growing instructions or important information (how long to germination, etc.) on the packet to help them along.

Store seeds carefully over the long term by placing envelopes inside large glass jars or boxes made of wood, cardboard, or tin. These materials will absorb excess moisture, while plastic will create moisture. Save those tiny bags of silica gel that come with new shoes and use them as an extra moisture-absorbing aid. Seeds stored in a cool, dry place should last for a few years, depending on the type. Taking extra measures now means less work next year.

## PUTTING THEM TO THE TEST

This seed-harvesting stuff might sound like a bother, but it's totally worth it. The majority of seed types will last a minimum of 3 years if stored correctly, so you need not go to the trouble every single year. In fact, many store-bought seeds last well past their due date, too. Before throwing old seed in the trash, do this simple low-tech test to check their reliability.

### Homemade Desiccant

Powdered milk sachets stored with seeds will absorb moisture and prevent mold from developing on your seeds. Pour 2 tablespoons of powdered milk into the center of a 5-inch square of cotton fabric or tissue paper. Pull the corners together and tie them together with a piece of string or elastic band. The sachet will continue to do its job for about 6 months. Once you're done with it, just dump it in the trash, or empty the milk onto your tomato plants.

**1.** Arrange 10 to 20 seeds of one type on one half of a sheet of moist paper towel.

**2.** Fold the sheet over with the seedless half touching the seeded half.

**3.** Fold or roll the towel and place inside a resealable plastic bag. Don't forget to label the bag so you know what's inside when you come back to it.

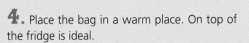
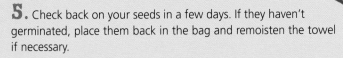

**4.** Place the bag in a warm place. On top of the fridge is ideal.

**5.** Check back on your seeds in a few days. If they haven't germinated, place them back in the bag and remoisten the towel if necessary.

**6.** Place the bag back in its comfy spot for a few more days.

**7.** Keep checking and remoistening the towel until seeds start to germinate. Count the number that have germinated and the number that haven't. If your success rate is around 50 percent, then you're good to go. If the percentage is lower, you can still use the seeds but should sow more come planting time to compensate for the loss. If they don't germinate, toss them out and hit up your seed-starting buddies for a fresh supply.

*This test can also be used to pregerminate difficult or old seed. Just pot up the towel-germinated seed as you would a regular seed. Pregerminating gives you an advantage because you'll know ahead of time if the seed is good or not.*

# SEED PACKETS

While you might want to resort to cheap 'n' easy envelopes for your private stash, homegrown organic seeds packaged in pretty decorative envelopes make a coveted gift for gardening friends. Flex your artistic muscles and fashion fancy packages from recycled paper.

**1.** Scan the envelope template found on page 201.

**2.** Print the scanned shape onto paper suitable for your at-home printer. Try semi-transparent vellum or colored or textured paper. As an alternative to scanning, photocopy the template onto paper of your choice.

**3.** Draw on or decorate the paper. If you're really going all out, draw quick sketches or add a photo of the plant the seeds came from.

**4.** Cut along the solid lines and fold along the dotted lines.

**5.** Dab glue where indicated and seal.

**6.** If you'd like, add a label to the front or write directly onto the envelope. Use fancy colored, gel, or metallic markers. Rub-on letters look good, too.

If you want to make a vintage-looking envelope or use found photos and images on your envelopes, take one more step. Since you won't be able to print directly onto paper scraps or recycled paper cut from magazines or old books, you'll need to make a traceable template.

**1.** Scan or photocopy the envelope template as described above.

**2.** Lay the design flat on the cutting mat and place a piece of Mylar on top. Tape down both the design and the Mylar to secure, then cut along the lines of the design with a sharp X-Acto knife. This is your stencil.

**3.** Lay the stencil over a sheet of unique paper. Trace along the outside with a pencil or pen.

## You Will Need

* Envelope template (see page 201)
* Paper for envelopes
* Materials for decorating
* X-Acto knife or scissors for cutting
* Cutting mat
* Ruler
* Paper glue
* 8½-by-11-inch sheet Mylar template plastic
* Tape
* Pencil or pen

**4.** Cut the envelope shape out.

**5.** Fold, glue, and seal.

**6.** If you'd like, add a label to the front or write directly onto the envelope.

## LABELS

Sticker labels gussy up plain envelopes and are necessary additions to envelopes made from recycled magazines and old books.

**1.** Scan a label template on page 200.

**2.** Print the scanned template onto an 8½-by-11-inch sheet of sticker paper. Office supply stores carry clear or opaque adhesive paper. As an alternative to scanning, photocopy the image directly onto sticker paper.

**3.** Cut the label out around the outside and adhere to the front of an assembled envelope.

*Sourcing Scrap Paper*

∗Used garden magazines
∗Old botanical or gardening books from garage sales, thrift stores, or library sales (bonus if you find books with illustrations or photos)
∗Decorative paper purchased from import stores
∗Used horticulture catalogs
∗All kinds of magazines

# YOUR BABIES MAKING BABIES

In an act of pure genius, nature gave plants the ability to clone themselves. You can put this magic to work for you to get full-fledged plants a whole lot faster and easier than growing from seeds. You can "clone" plants by either division or from cuttings.

## DIVISION

It sounds just like what it is: plants are dug up and "divided" into smaller plants. Even if you don't want more plants, most perennials that grow in clumps (grasses, yarrow, lilies) become miserable and droopy when their space is maxed out. Dividing produces an army of clone babies and gives old plants a new lease on life.

Midsummer is the best time to work on dividing spring-flowering bulbs or irises that have finished blooming. Early fall and spring are optimum times to confront most overgrown perennials. Choose a rainy or damp day to go for it when wet soil is loose and easier to dig up.

Carefully dig around midsized plants or lift manageable chunks of mammoth plants from the soil with a spade. Carefully disentangle roots by hand or cut through hard clumps with a sharp knife. Replant the healthiest plants in a new spot, leaving space for new growth. Pot up any remaining healthy plants to give to friends and compost the dead, dry chunks.

Approach the task with an ounce of care. Most plants are hardy and can take a little prodding. However, torn stems and roots can introduce pathogens into the plant and prevent a speedy recovery.

## Natural Rooting Hormone

When rooting cuttings in water, you can speed up the process without synthetic hormones by placing a piece of willow branch in the water along with the cutting. Willow contains natural auxins, hormones that stimulate root growth and development.

## Supersize Your Basil

Around midsummer, you can root pieces of basil cut from the bushy plants that are already established in your garden. Carefully cut 4-inch-long pieces of your healthy basil plants. Place the cuttings in a jar or glass filled with fresh water and set it away from hot sunlight. In about a week you'll have rooted plants ready to be potted up or planted in the garden.

The best part is that you can share cuttings with friends to expand your basil collection to include unusual varieties that are hard to grow or don't grow from seed at all, such as sacred basil or African blue basil.

# CUTTINGS

Cuttings are a miracle method for propagating your favorite annual and perennial plants. Geraniums, chrysanthemums, and fuchsias are just a few candidates for easy duplication by cuttings. Rooting a cutting can be as simple as placing some stems of basil or mint from the grocery store or the garden into a container of water!

I stay prepared and keep a small pair of scissors and a sandwich bag in my handbag at all times, in case I find some super-potent catnip growing in a field or a pretty scented geranium missing from my collection. When I see something fabulous in someone's yard, I ring the bell and ask if I can clip a bit of the owner's plant. Gardeners are always happy to share. If you're going to sneak a clipping, play fair and take care rather than grabbing and yanking a chunk off the host plant.

Choose healthy plants that are free of disease or insect infestations. Problems will only spread from the parent plant to the new babies.

## To Root Cuttings in Water

**1.** Using a good pair of sharp scissors, make a clean, crisp angled cut just below the node (the juncture on the stem where the leaves are attached).

**2.** Remove the lower leaves, creating a bare stem that is 2 to 4 inches from the base.

**3.** Place in a glass or jar of water. In a few days the stems will produce roots. If it doesn't produce roots in 5 days, make a fresh cut and try again.

**4.** Once the roots are at least ½ inch long, pot up your cutting in potting soil appropriate for the plant.

## To Root Cuttings in Soil

**1.** Repeat steps 1 and 2 of To Root Cuttings in Water.

**2.** Dip the fresh-cut end of the stem in rooting hormone. Rooting hormone is a product (available as a powder or gel) that promotes root growth. It often also contains fungicides that protect the stem from rotting before it can produce roots.

**3.** Fill a small plastic pot with potting soil.

**4.** Make a 2-inch-deep hole in the soil with a pencil or your finger. Place the cutting in the hole, making sure you don't disturb the rooting hormone.

**5.** Press the soil down around the cutting and water thoroughly.

**6.** Keep the soil consistently moist until the cutting has established roots and has resumed growing.

Rooted cuttings make great gifts for fellow gardeners. Pot up a piece of your prized nutmeg geranium or favorite coleus in a cute thrift-score container for an added touch. Trading cuttings with gardening pals is a fast way to increase your plant collection. Gardeners are always keen to exchange excess plants for new flora. This past year I made a quick swap with an anonymous gardener who was driving by as I dug up excess daylilies from my street-side garden. Just when I was starting to worry about what I'd do with all the extras, she happened by with a clump of beautiful silver-leaved yarrow in the backseat! Tit for tat and everyone's happy.

*make an angled cut below the node*

*dip in rooting hormone*

*make a two-inch deep hole*

# CHILL

Okay, winter is a huge drag. Even though I know it is an important part of the natural cycle of life, I can't help but resent the brutal cold and the months locked indoors. I have to remind myself that winter can also be a nice break. It provides a perfect opportunity to look back on what happened during the season and fantasize about next year. Even if you live in a climate that doesn't force you to wear a giant down jacket for six months straight, your garden will still experience seasonal change and periods of rest.

So exactly what do you do to prepare your garden for the long (or short) winter haul? This section covers the basics of preparing and winding down your garden for winter as well as inspiring ideas to maintain momentum while you wait for the next gardening season to gear up.

# REFLECTIONS

Use the time away from garden demands to reflect on your successes and challenges during the growing season. Curl up in a comfy chair with a hot cup of homegrown herbal tea (or if you're in Los Angeles, with a cup of iced tea) and dream about how much your garden is going to kick butt next year. Your answers to the following questions will reveal a path for next year.

* Did you use your garden?
* Was there somewhere comfortable to sit and enjoy it?
* Did your plants look healthy and happy overall?
* Which plants thrived?
* Which didn't?
* Which diseases appeared more than once?
* Which insect pests caused a ruckus?
* Which plants were too hard to maintain?
* Were there bare spots or periods when nothing was in bloom?
* Which plant groupings worked well together?
* Which part of your garden was your favorite?
* What aspect drove you crazy with frustration?

## CH-CH-CHANGES

Don't be afraid to make changes in the garden. If something ain't right, it's better to rip it out now rather than waste time and space hoping it will magically improve itself down the road.

* **Follow Your Heart**—Did anything inspire you that you would like to try in your garden? Think about how you can incorporate a new idea or elements of it into your space. Even if an idea looks too expensive or out of your league, bits and pieces might work for you.

* **If It Ain't Broke**—Do more of what worked. In fact, do lots and lots of it. Don't worry about becoming a one-trick pony. Success is a gateway drug to the harder stuff. It makes you feel good, providing encouragement to take on bigger challenges and try new things.

* **Problem Solve**—Look at what didn't work in the past, especially consistent, recurring problems. What can you do to fix them? Sometimes the answer is simple. If a plant isn't working in one spot, move it. Perhaps a certain plant just doesn't suit your environment. Try to find something similar that does work, or scrap it entirely and start fresh.

## GET TO LEARNING

Some learn by doing, others learn by reading and communing with others. All that extra leisure time in the off-season gives you the perfect opportunity to leaf through the gardening books and magazines that sat neglected during the busy gardening months. It also offers a chance to reach out to other plant lovers who are also suffering from garden separation anxiety. Horticultural groups often slow down during the winter, but online groups and gardening bulletin boards are on fire with gardeners desperate to talk shop. Reach out, compare notes, or start an online journal and show off a bit.

# GARDEN MEMORY JOURNAL

A garden journal can serve a variety of purposes. Some record facts and details of the gardening process: you can include snips of plant material, garden tags, diagrams, and charts to keep track of garden activity, strategies, and schemes. Other journals are memory containers, reflecting moments of triumph and defeat in your garden. Making your own journal provides a personalized connection to your green space and is a great project for the cold days of winter.

With a few tools and a crafty constitution, you can make a stylish and functional journal like the ones pictured here.

**1.** Using a sharp X-Acto knife, remove the front and back covers from the spine of the book. Make your cuts right at the edge of the hardcover board. For the following directions, I will assume that your book covers are 8 inches wide by 10 inches high. But yours can be any size at all!

**2.** Cut 2 pieces of mill board to 1½ inches wide by the height of your book covers (8 by 10 inches). These will be your spines. Use board that is the approximate thickness of your book cover.

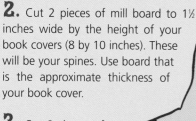

**3.** Cut 2 sheets of decorative paper as lining for the inside of your front and back covers. These are called endpapers. Endpapers are traditionally inset slightly from the margins of the cover for a polished look. To achieve this effect, cut them ¼ inch smaller than your cover. In my example, the endpapers are 7½ inches by 9½ inches in size. You can use the preexisting endpapers as a guide. Since you will be gluing your papers on top of the existing endpapers, choose an opaque paper.

## You Will Need

* An old hardcover book
* X-Acto knife
* Cutting mat
* Wide paintbrush
* Mill board (aka bookbinding board)
* Steel ruler
* Decorative paper for endpapers (opaque)
* PVA glue (I like Good Glue)
* Bone folder
* Bookcloth
* Pinking shears
* Drill
* ¼ inch drill bit
* Several large sheets of opaque paper (at least 26 inches by 22 inches each) for pages
* Hole punch (single hole)
* 3 Chicago bolts (aka screw posts)
* Envelopes

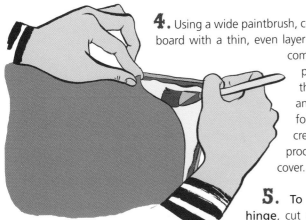

**4.** Using a wide paintbrush, coat the inside of each board with a thin, even layer of glue. Once it becomes tacky, lay the end paper in position onto the inside front cover and rub with a bone folder to remove all creases. Repeat the process for the back cover.

**5.** To create the book hinge, cut a piece of bookcloth that is 5½ inches wide and 3 inches longer than the length of your book cover. In my example, that would be 5½ inches by 13 inches.

**6.** Using pinking shears, cut a decorative edge down the length of the bookcloth on both sides.

**7.** Apply a coat of PVA glue to the paper-backed side of your bookcloth. Lay the front cover of your book 1½ inches from the right edge of the cloth. The cover should be centered vertically.

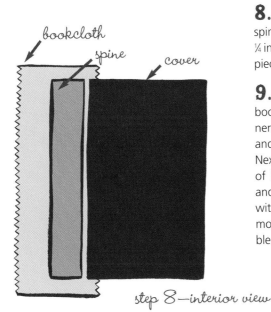

bookcloth

spine

cover

*step 8—interior view*

**8.** Position one of the spines next to the cover with ¼ inch distance between the pieces.

**9.** Fold the corners of the bookcloth up toward the corners of the cover on an angle and glue down securely. Next, fold the bottom flaps of bookcloth onto the cover and secure with glue. Rub with the bone folder to remove all creases and air bubbles.

*Books*

Thrift stores, garage sales, church rummage sales, and library discard shelves are great places to find vintage hardcover books cheap. Look for books with an interesting cover that's in good shape. The inside content and paper quality is irrelevant. Check underneath paper covers for embossed designs. Some old books are even covered with cloth rather than paper which works fine, too.

*Design Ideas*

There are lots of ways to make this simple journal template your own. Chicago bolts come in a variety of colors and materials from clear plastic to anodized aluminium. Place sheets of translucent Mylar, tissue paper, or cool pages torn from old magazines and books intermittently throughout the book as pretty section dividers. Use stamps or rub-on letters for text. Punch holes into envelopes and bind them right into the book for storing seeds, tags, leaves, or other bits collected in the garden. You can even make your own paper and drop in some flower petals from your garden. Hand sew or glue pretty seed packets or photos of your plants to the pages of your book.

**10.** Finally, fold the remaining bookcloth over to encase the spine. Apply glue and rub with the bone folder.

**11.** Repeat steps 5 to 10 to make the back cover.

**12.** Using a ¼-inch drill bit, drill three holes into the front cover spine. Position the holes at an equal distance apart along the length of the spine and ½ inch from the left edge.

**13.** Line your front cover up with your back cover and mark the holes with a pencil. Drill each hole in the back cover spine.

**14.** To make the pages for your book, you will first need to take measurements of your cover to determine the size the pages should be. For width, measure from the very edge of the spine to the edge of the endpaper on the opposite side. The length should be the length of the endpaper. Double the measurement of the width for your final size: e.g., if your width is 8 inches and your book length is 10 inches, your final sheet size should be 16 inches wide by 10 inches long.

**15.** Cut large sheets of paper down to the measurements determined above. Once cut, stack 5 sheets into a pile and fold in half. This group is called a "signature." Repeat until you have a total of 5 signatures.

**16.** Lay the front cover on top of your stack of signatures and mark the drill holes with a pencil. Drill through the stack of signatures. A hole punch will do the job, too.

**17.** Now all that's left to do is assemble your pieces and close up the screw posts.

*step 10—interior view*

*Pretty Paper*

Rather than buying fancy paper for lining your book, recycle interesting sheets from old books. Look for vintage encyclopedias and gardening books with lots of illustrations or supersaturated photographs of flowers and gardening ladies.

# MAKE YOUR OWN BOOKCLOTH

Bookcloth is an expensive, specialized bookbinding material that is difficult to find and comes only in limited colors. It is only available from specialty bookbinding or paper shops. Making your own is easy and way cooler anyway. Use scraps of gorgeous vintage fabric, bark cloth, and cotton, or cut up old clothes that don't fit anymore. Japanese lining paper, called kozo, is traditionally used as backing, but any paper on the thin side (similar to a cheap bond paper) will do.

**1.** Cut a piece of thin paper that is 2 inches larger than your fabric piece on all sides.

**2.** Lay down a sheet of kraft paper to protect your work surface. Do not use newspaper as it may transfer ink to the fabric.

**3.** Using a wide paintbrush, completely cover the paper in glue.

**4.** Set it aside for a few minutes until it becomes tacky.

**5.** Lay the piece of fabric (good side up) onto the glued paper and gently rub it down with your fingers.

**6.** Using the bone folder, continue to rub the fabric down, removing creases. Be careful not to allow glue to penetrate through the fabric.

**7.** Turn the entire piece over so that the paper side is now facing up. Continue to rub the paper with the bone folder. This action actually stretches the paper a bit more.

**8.** Once dry, trim down the paper edges. You've got book cloth!

> ## You Will Need
>
> * Thin paper (or Japanese kozo)
> * Kraft paper
> * Wide paintbrush
> * PVA glue (I like Good Glue)
> * Piece of fabric
> * Bone folder

# ALL THE LEAVES ARE BROWN

If you're lucky enough to live in a region that does not experience a cold, frosty winter, you may have the option of gardening all year round. Northern gardeners experience gardening as a season with a beginning and an end. But in some climates winter means cooler, chilly, wetter, or dryer rather than get-inside-before-you-turn-to-ice! In these climates, gardening doesn't have to come to an abrupt end but rather slows down or simply changes. This could mean that when some of us are hibernating, moderate-climate and southern climate gardeners are getting ready to start a new crop or preparing to protect the garden from tropical storms rather than flurries and deep freezes.

In tropical and subtropical climates summer can be too hot for some veggie crops but cooler seasons will be just right. This is downright backward to a northern gardener like me, and I admit to a touch of envy. In south Florida, winter means less humidity and oppressive heat—considered by many to be the perfect time to start a veggie crop.

Get to know your climate and find out what's possible. Again, it's often a simple matter of looking around at what your neighbors are doing. It pays to be nosy. Of course it's up to you if you'd rather take a nice, relaxing break like the rest of us and come back to gardening refreshed and reenergized. Just because three or four crops a year is possible doesn't mean you absolutely must hustle and sweat year-round.

## FALL PRUNING

✷ Climbers must be pruned back to protect them from harsh winter winds and heavy snowfalls that will break fragile stems. All that exposed foliage is susceptible to damage.

✷ Grasses, tough herbs, and thick-stemmed perennials can be left uncut to keep a speck of life in the garden during a harsh winter. Dogwood branches and perennial seedpods look pretty poking out through the snow. Extra foliage holds snow in the garden. Surprisingly, that's a good thing! Snow acts as extra insulation to protect plants from the bitter cold. Remember, it's not the snow that damages plants, but the repeated thawing and refreezing.

✷ If you live in a climate that doesn't experience snowy winters, you can lay off the fall pruning or use fall as an opportunity to reshape, cut back, and generally tidy up unruly, end-of-season plants.

## Late-Season Crops

Grow these plants when the temperature has cooled down and you don't want the summer blooming to end. Depending on your climate, cooling temperatures can come in early fall or as late as January.

**To eat:** Lettuce greens, radish, arugula, kale, spinach
**Flowers:** Chrysanthemums, pansies, violas, asters

# THE BIG CHILL

Fall, just before the first frost kicks in, is the time to begin getting your garden geared up for the long haul through winter. Here's where the question of tender or hardy becomes really important. Hardy plants and bulbs, just like the name says, are hardy enough to tough it out through a frozen northern winter. Tender plants and bulbs can't hack a frost and need to either be brought indoors for the winter or left out and sacrificed to the elements. Any tender annuals are done for anyway, so no need to bring them inside. But tender perennials that you want to live to see another year will need an indoor vacation. Some plants are semi-hardy and sometimes need a little extra protection over the winter.

If you live in a climate that doesn't experience frost or freeze, you'll be spared a lot of this buttoning-down work. Focus on the tidying up and seasonal transition, but all your plants, whether tender or hardy, will make it through the frost-free winter outside.

The fall gear-up is about protection, prevention, and tidiness.

## IN-GROUND GARDENS

✻ Start your winter prep by bringing tender potted plants indoors well before the first frost. Dig up tender perennials that have been growing in the ground all season, pot them, and bring them inside with the rest.

✻ Removing diseased plants should be priority number two. Diseases lay dormant through the cold winter months only to come back twofold as soon as the heat is on. Just pull up and chuck any diseased plants, whether they're annuals or perennials.

✻ Now's your chance to do a light cleanup in the garden. Gather up those extra, unused stakes; rake up leaves and pruned foliage; sweep up the piles of potting soil you dropped in a midsummer frenzy. Messes only get worse during a wet, cold winter.

✻ Annual plants (flowers or veggies) that are merely past their prime can stay or go depending on your personal taste. Some gardeners rip out all their annuals at the end of the season, but I think a few plants left in the garden prevent soil erosion and provide a place for animals to live (a good or bad thing, depending on your perspective). As plant material breaks down throughout the course of the winter, the humus content of your soil multiplies—instant soil building! Of course, any hardy in-ground perennials will also stay out for the winter, but what to do with your annuals is up to you.

*Winter Crops*

*Dig up herbs, pot them up, and place them indoors in a sunny window. A few plants will provide you with fresh cooking herbs all winter long.*

* Protecting semi-hardy plants (such as tea roses) that can't take harsh winter weather is boring but necessary work in cold climates. Cover them with a layer of burlap, gather it loosely around the base, and tie with twine so it doesn't fly away in winter winds. Burlap is available at garden stores or fabric stores for really cheap. You can also add an extra layer of mulch for additional protection.

If you live in a climate that doesn't normally have a frost, you don't need to bother with this. But if you hear reports of a freak frost coming in the middle of winter, put on your gardening gear and jump into the yard to cover those plants. If you don't have burlap lying around, use old sheets or even big towels. Secure fabric loosely with rope or twine and cross your fingers.

* Hardy native plants will do just fine without extra protection or fuss. I neglected cleanup almost entirely last year, all under the guise of "experimentation," of course. The only plant that didn't come back with a vengeance was a 3-year-old English lavender. Everything else was fine. Tall grasses and tough perennials (*sedum* 'Autumn Joy', black-eyed Susan) peeking up through the snow provide something extra to look at over the winter months besides a sea of white.

## POTTED GARDENS

You can kick your feet up and skip this part if your climate doesn't succumb to long-term freezes. The rest of us need to take a few extra precautions in order to preserve the life of our potted plants.

* Potted gardens are less forgiving than the in-ground kind. Payback for an afternoon of videos and hot cocoa when you should be out cleaning terra-cotta pots is a mess of broken clay and ceramic shards come spring. That vintage McCoy planter after a winter outside—toast. If you live in a climate that freezes, you'll either need to bring the pots indoors or take the plants out of any terra-cotta or ceramic pots, toss the plants into the compost heap, empty the soil out and save it for next year, then follow the directions below for cleaning pots and bring them indoors.

If indoor space is hard to come by, keep your regular clay pots (not the fancy ones) in a sheltered place like a garage or shed where they will get some protection from the elements. Expanding and contracting moisture is the real culprit behind terra-cotta destruction. As long as they're kept dry, your pots should be okay.

Most plants, even the hardy ones, won't survive a deep freeze in a small pot. Planter boxes are deep enough to sustain perennials and bulbs year-round. If it's not in a big container or planter box, bring it in.

### How to Clean Pots

**1.** Soak dirty pots in a sink or tub filled with warm, soapy water. Add a splash of oxygenated bleach (hydrogen peroxide) to sanitize.

**2.** Scrub well with a wire brush. Don't forget to get inside the nooks and crannies.

**3.** Thoroughly rinse pots with clean water to remove all traces of soap and hydrogen peroxide.

**4.** Set aside on a dish rack to dry.

## How to Bring Them Inside

Rather than leaving nonhardy plants outdoors to brave the elements or chucking them in the compost bin, bring them inside. Rosemary, scented geraniums, lemon verbena, and tender sages (tangerine and pineapple) can be enjoyed indoors throughout the winter and placed right back outside come spring. Bring tender plants in just before the first expected frost date to avoid disaster. Check the *Farmer's Almanac* for predicted first frost dates in your area (see Resources).

✱ Choose only the healthiest plants to bring inside. There's no point to overwintering a sick plant.

✱ Don't bring insect pests indoors with your plants. Give your plants a thorough inspection. Don't forget to look under leaves. Sprinkle a bit of diatomaceous earth on the soil surface if soil-dwelling critters are suspected. Pull plants out of their containers and inspect the roots for extra insurance.

✱ Prune back some of the leaves and stem. This will help the plant adapt to new lighting conditions.

If plants have grown too large for your space, take cuttings rather than bringing the entire plant indoors. Geraniums, coleus, and fuchsia are good candidates for this clip-n-toss method.

## KEEPING THEM COLD

Even cold-hardy plants that normally withstand freezing temperatures can suffer serious damage when the winter freeze doesn't stick. Cold-hardy plants adapt to a deep freeze by shutting down into a dormant stage. Problems occur when the weather temporarily warms up, thawing frozen soil. When the soil refreezes, it expands, shifting plants up toward the surface, sometimes exposing tender roots to freezing temperatures. This is called "heaving."

Temporary, premature thaws can also prompt plants out of the dormant stage under the pretense that spring has sprung and it's time to get growing. All that new growth is tender and susceptible to serious damage when the weather turns back to freezing again.

To protect your plants from the seesaw freeze-thaw-refreeze, apply a heavy layer of mulch after the ground has frozen. Rather than keeping the plants warm, this mulch will keep the soil frozen during temporary thaws.

## SALT PROTECTION

Salt is a serious winter problem in the city. Curbside plants tend to get salted by passing cars and road-salting machines, never mind well-meaning neighbors and landlords. Salt is a powerful herbicide that can seriously burn, damage, and even kill plants. To protect yours, apply a layer of plastic over the soil in areas that are likely to get hit. If salt does get on the plants or soil, water the soil well come spring (unless there is ample rain). The water will leach salt through the soil quickly and minimize damage.

# HERE COMES THE SUN

Beat the late-winter blahs and bring a little bit of spring cheer indoors. Branches cut from early season flowering trees such as cherry, apple, forsythia, and pussy willow will burst into bloom when placed in a jar of water in the house.

**1.** Wait for a mild winter day to go out branch collecting. The temperature can be above or below freezing, but the warmer the better. February and March are the best months for most trees. The closer to the plant's actual blooming time, the faster your branches will flower.

**2.** Choose long, medium-width branches with lots of plump buds. Each bud will become a flower, so more buds equals maximum blooms.

**3.** Make a diagonal cut about ¼ inch above the base of the stem.

**4.** Once inside, recut the stems and make a second vertical cut on the underside of the branch along the cut end. Immediately place the branch in a large jar of lukewarm water.

**5.** Place your jar or vase in a cool location away from direct sunlight. It can take from a few days to a few weeks for buds to open. Change the water every few days to prevent mold from forming and rotting the stems.

Trimming a few branches for indoor enjoyment won't harm the tree as long as you use sharp clippers for a clean cut and don't take too many branches from one tree.

## Get Some

If you don't have your own backyard bushes or trees, look for bundled branches left for roadside pickup. Most people don't realize the potential for their discarded prunings. Or ask a neighbor who has plenty of trees if you can take a few branches.

## You Will Need

* Branches
* Pruning shears
* Large jar or vase
* Lukewarm water (the temperature of warm water out of the tap)

## Try These Branches for Forcing

* Apple
* Cherry
* Forsythia
* Lilac
* Magnolia
* Peach
* Pussy willow
* Witch hazel

# WINTER PREP CHECKLIST

Winter might mean 3-foot drifts of snow where you are, or merely some chilly, rainy days with a slight chance of frost. But in any climate, there comes a time when you need to clean up, button up, and prep the garden for some down time.

## IN THE GARDEN

☐ Prune back climbing or vining plants.

☐ Remove all diseased foliage.

☐ Apply fresh organic compost to beds that need a boost.

☐ Dig up and remove tender bulb plants such as dahlias or gladioli.

☐ Rake leaves where they have piled up too thickly. Make them into leaf mold (see page 48 for instructions).

☐ Lay a 1-inch layer of mulch over your garden bed. Be sure to add extra around roses, lavender, strawberries, and other tender perennials.

☐ Clean tools before tucking them away for winter (see page 67). Bring them indoors if you don't have a shed or other dry place to keep them.

## ON THE DECK OR PATIO

☐ Compost all dead plant material or plants that will not go inside for the winter.

☐ Clean your pots. Store them inside a shed or indoors away from extreme temperatures (see sidebar on page 186 for instructions).

☐ Wrap up tender trees with burlap.

# GLOSSARY

**Annual**—A plant that completes its life cycle in one growing season, beginning as a seed, then flowering, and finally producing new seed before dying.

**Biennial**—A plant that completes its life cycle in two growing seasons. It develops leaves in the first season and spends the second season producing flowers, and finally seeds, before dying.

**Bolting**—When plants produce flowers and seeds prematurely due to extreme weather conditions. Hot sun and heat are common factors.

**Cloche**—A miniature greenhouse device used to protect an individual plant or seedling from harsh weather conditions.

**Cross-pollination**—The transfer of pollen from one flower to a flower on another plant.

**Family**—One group used in classifying organisms. Families consist of a number of similar genera.

**Genus (plural: genera)**—In plant classification, a group of species of plants that are closely related to one another.

**Hardy**—Hardiness refers to how much cold or freezing weather a plant can tolerate. A hardy plant can survive a cold winter outdoors.

**Heaving**—Heaving occurs when the soil expands and contracts as frozen soil thaws and refreezes. This causes plants to shift up toward the soil surface where their roots are susceptible to freezing temperatures.

**Heirloom**—A plant variety that has remained unchanged in an area for at least fifty to one hundred years. They are always open pollinated.

**Humus**—Decomposed plant matter that is part of the soil.

**Hybrid**—A plant variety resulting from the controlled crossbreeding between two plants of the same or closely related species that have distinct characteristics. Plants are usually crossbred under controlled conditions to create very specific results.

**Nematode**—Parasitic worms that can prey on animals or plants. The garden variety are microscopic.

**Open pollinated**—A plant variety whose seeds develop as the result of random, natural pollination.

**Ornamental**—A plant that is grown for its beauty. Ornamentals often have special characteristics such as colorful leaves that set them apart from average varieties.

**Perennial**—A plant that lives for more than two seasons and does not die after flowering. Most perennials die back to the soil surface at the end of each growing season and come up again at the beginning of the next season.

**Pinching off**—Periodically removing the new, fresh growth from a leafy plant to encourage bushy growth. It is called "pinching off" because the tender growth can be removed by pinching with your fingers.

**Pot up**—To plant in a container or pot.

**Propagation**—To multiply a plant by various methods, such as division or taking cuttings.

**Pumice**—Frothy volcanic rock used as an ingredient in container soil mix.

**Self-pollinator**—A plant whose individual flowers contain all the necessary parts to successfully pollinate themselves.

**Self-sowing**—When a plant produces seeds and germinates without human assistance.

**Side dressing**—A method of fertilizing in which a little fertilizer is worked into the soil alongside a mature plant.

**Species**—In plant classification, a group of plants with common characteristics that can crossbreed with one another.

**Suckers**—A stem that develops in the crotch between the main stem and a leaf. They are also known as "side shoots."

**Tender**—A plant that cannot survive frost conditions.

**Variety**—A subcategory of a species that has slightly different but inheritable characteristics. Such characteristics include differing leaf color or shape.

**Volunteer**—A plant that pops up in a place where it hasn't been planted intentionally. Most volunteers are the result of self-seeding.

# RESOURCES

## BODY FOOD

Ingredients such as cocoa butter, beeswax, and sweet almond oil can be purchased at your local health food store.
Metal tins and packaging: www.sunburstbottle.com

## CARNIVOROUS PLANTS

*Information:*

* The Carnivorous Plants FAQ: www.sarracenia.com/faq.html
* International Carnivorous Plant Society: www.carnivorousplants.org
* *The Savage Garden*, Peter D'Amato (1998, Ten Speed Press)

*Get Some:*

* Botanique: www.pitcherplant.com
* California Carnivores: www.californiacarnivores.com

## COMMUNITY GARDENING

* American Community Garden Association: www.communitygarden.org
* Green Thumb: www.greenthumbnyc.org
* *How Does Our Garden Grow? A Guide to Community Garden Success*, by Laura Berman (1997, Toronto Community Garden Network: www.foodshare.net)

## COMPANION PLANTING

* *Carrots Love Tomatoes*, Louise Riotte (1998, Storey Publishing)
* *Great Garden Companions*, Sally Jean Cunningham (2000, Rodale Books)

## COMPOSTING

* *Let It Rot: The Gardener's Guide to Composting*, Stu Campbell (1998, Storey Publishing)
* *Soil and Composting: The Complete Guide to Building Healthy, Fertile Soil*, Nancy J. Ondra and Barbara Ellis (1998, Houghton Mifflin Co.)
* *The Worm Book: The Complete Guide to Worms in Your Garden*, Loren Nancarrow and Janet Hogan Taylor (1998, Ten Speed Press)
* *Worms Eat My Garbage*, Mary Appelhof (1982, Flower Press)

# EDIBLE FOOD GARDENING

* *The Edible Flower Garden*, Rosalind Creasy (1999, Periplus Editions)
* *Herbal: The Essential Guide to Herbs for Living*, Deni Bown (2001, Pavilion Books Limited)
* *How to Grow More Vegetables Than You Ever Thought Possible on Less Land Than You Can Imagine*, John Jeavons (1995, Ten Speed Press)
* *How to Grow Vegetables & Fruits by the Organic Method*, edited by J. I. Rodale and Staff (1961 and 1999, Rodale Press)
* *New Kitchen Garden: Organic Gardening and Cooking with Herbs, Vegetables and Fruit*, Adam Caplin (2003, Ryland Peters & Small Ltd.)
* *The Vegetable Gardener's Bible*, Edward Smith (2000, Storey Books)

# FUN STUFF

* Desktop Plant: http://downloads-zdnet.com. (Search under "desktop plant") — Grow a virtual plant on your computer desktop.
* Garden with Insight: www.gardenwithinsight.com—Garden simulation software.

# GARDEN DESIGN AND MANAGEMENT

* *Artists in Their Gardens*, Valerie Easton (2001, Sasquatch Books)
* Cactofilia (Free Software): www.cactofilia.com
* *Garden Decoration from Junk*, Leeann MacKenzie (2000, Collins & Brown)
* My Garden Journal: www.mygardenjournal.com—30-day free trial
* Virtual Garden Maker (Free Software): www.bbc.co.uk/gardening/design/virtual garden_index.shtml

# GARDEN PESTS

* *The Audubon Society Field Guide to North American Insects and Spiders*, Lorus Milne and Margery Milne (1980, Alfred A. Knopf)
* *The Organic Gardener's Handbook of Natural Insect and Disease Control*, edited by Barbara W. Ellis and Fern Marshall Bradley (1996, Rodale Press)

## ONLINE JOURNALING

* Blogger: www.blogger.com
* Live Journal: www.livejournal.com
* Movable Type: www.movabletype.org
* Text Pattern: www.textpattern.com
* Type Pad: www.typepad.com
* Word Press: www.wordpress.org

## PHOTOS

* Flickr: www.flickr.com
* Digital Photography Review: www.dpreview.com

## REGIONAL GARDENING

### Northern

* *Care-Free Plants: A Guide to Grow the 200 Hardiest Low-Maintenance, Long-Living Beauties* (2002, Reader's Digest)
* I Can Garden: www.icangarden.com
* The Renegade Gardener: www.renegadegardener.com

### Southeast

* *Complete Guide to Florida Gardening*, Stan Defreitas (2002, Taylor Trade Publishing)
* Southern Gardening: www.southerngardening.com

### Southwest

* *Gardening in the Desert: A Guide to Plant Selection and Care*, Mary Irish (2000, University of Arizona Press)
* *Nevada Gardener's Guide*, Linn Mills (2001, Cool Springs Press)

## West Coast

* *Gardening with Native Plants of the Pacific Northwest*, Arthur R. Kruckeberg (1997, University of Washington Press)
* *Gardening with a Wild Heart: Restoring California's Native Landscapes at Home*, Judith Larner Lowry (1999, University of California Press)
* *The Northwest Gardener's Resource Directory*, Stephanie Feeney (2002, Sasquatch Books)
* Slugs and Salal: www.slugsandsalal.com (Pacific Northwest Gardening)
* *Sunset Western Garden Book*, Kathleen Norris Brenzel (2001, Sunset Publishing Corporation)

## SOIL TESTING

Contact your county Extension Office (found in your phone book).

## TRADING SEEDS AND PLANTS

Check your local or national department of agriculture or customs office for current laws and regulations.

### In the United States

* Animal and Plant Health Inspection Service (APHIS): www.aphis.usda.gov

### In Canada

* Agriculture and Agri-Food Canada: www.agr.gc.ca
* Canadian Food Inspection Agency: www.inspection.gc.ca for a phytosanitary certificate

### Trading in the United States

* Garden State Heirloom Seed Society: www.historyyoucaneat.org
* Seed Savers Exchange: www.seedsavers.org
* Seed Savers' Network: www.seedsavers.net

### Trading in Canada

* Seeds of Diversity Canada: www.seeds.ca

## SEED PURCHASE

* Burpee: www.burpee.com
* The Cook's Garden: www.cooksgarden.com
* Johnny's Selected Seeds: www.johnnyseeds.com
* Seeds of Change: www.seedsofchange.com
* Stokes Seeds: www.stokeseeds.com
* Urban Harvest: www.uharvest.ca
* Veseys Seeds Ltd.: www.veseys.com

## URBAN AND CONTAINER GARDENING:

* *The Edible Container Garden*, Michael Guerra (2000, Simon and Schuster)
* *Planted*, Andy Sturgeon (1998, Hodder & Stoughton)
* *Urban Eden*, Adam and James Caplin (2000, Kyle Cathie Limited)

## MISCELLANEOUS

* *Biomimicry: Innovation Inspired by Nature*, Janine M. Benyus (1997, Perennial)
* *Botany for Gardeners: An Introduction and Guide*, Brian Capon (1990, Timber Press)
* *The Botany of Desire: A Plant's-Eye View of the World*, Michael Pollan (2001, Random House)
* Cobra Head Precision Weeder and Cultivator: www.cobrahead.com
* *Eat More Dirt: Diverting and Instructive Tips for Growing and Tending an Organic Garden*, Ellen Sandbeck (2003, Broadway Books)
* *Encyclopedia of Organic Gardening*, Edited by J. I. Rodale and Staff (1959, Rodale Press)
* Farmers' Almanac: www.farmersalmanac.com
* Garden Web: www.gardenweb.com
* *Landscaping Revolution: Gardening with Nature Not Against Her*, Andy and Sally Wasowski (2000, Contemporary Books)
* *Making More Plants: The Science, Art, and Joy of Propagation*, Ken Druse (2000, Clarkson Potter)
* *The Natural Habitat Garden*, Ken Druse (1994, Clarkson Potter)

# USDA PLANT HARDINESS ZONE MAP

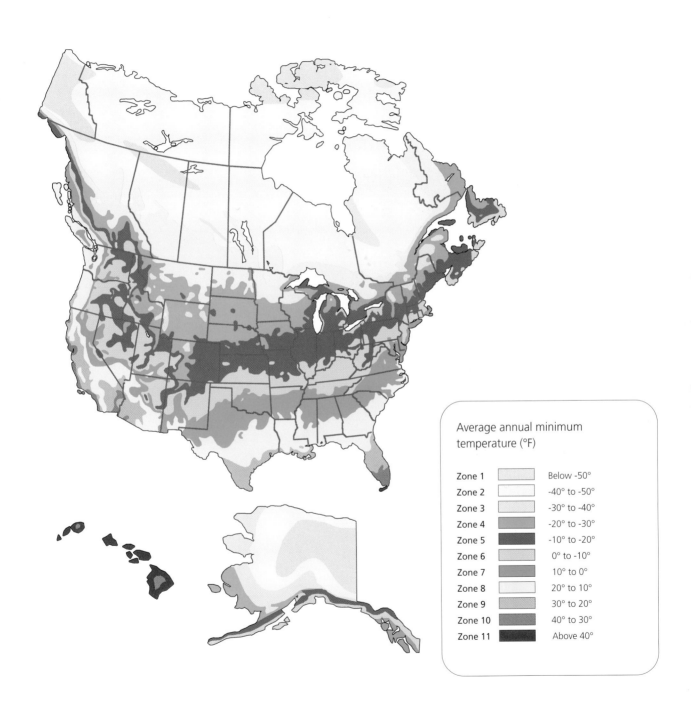

Average annual minimum
temperature (°F)

|  |  |
|------|-------------|
| Zone 1 | Below -50° |
| Zone 2 | -40° to -50° |
| Zone 3 | -30° to -40° |
| Zone 4 | -20° to -30° |
| Zone 5 | -10° to -20° |
| Zone 6 | 0° to -10° |
| Zone 7 | 10° to 0° |
| Zone 8 | 20° to 10° |
| Zone 9 | 30° to 20° |
| Zone 10 | 40° to 30° |
| Zone 11 | Above 40° |

# SEED PACKET TEMPLATES

TEMPLATES

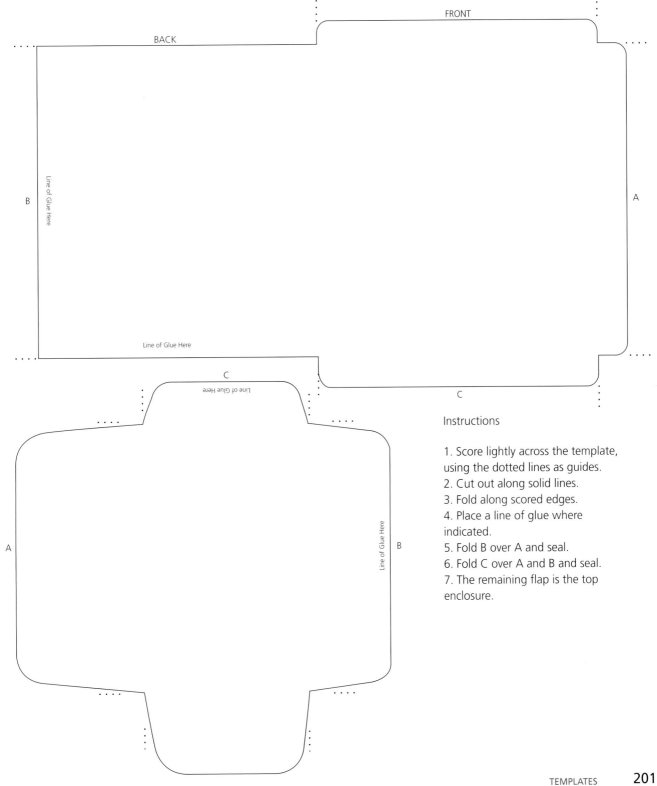

BACK

FRONT

B

Line of Glue Here

A

Line of Glue Here

C

C

A

Line of Glue Here

C

Line of Glue Here

B

Instructions

1. Score lightly across the template, using the dotted lines as guides.
2. Cut out along solid lines.
3. Fold along scored edges.
4. Place a line of glue where indicated.
5. Fold B over A and seal.
6. Fold C over A and B and seal.
7. The remaining flap is the top enclosure.

# CHALKBOARD POT TEMPLATES

# INDEX

# CREDITS

## COVER ILLUSTRATION

Leela Corman

## BOOK ILLUSTRATIONS

Leela Corman

## PHOTO CREDITS

Gayla Trail
With:
pp. 9, 16, 37, 54, 61, 67 (top), 69, 75, 77, 135, 140, 152, 167, 175, 189 (top right), 208: Davin Risk
p. 22: Mark Wickham
p. 143 (lavender): Lee Pettet / iStockphoto
p. 158 (aloe vera): Stephanie Asher / iStockphoto

## DESIGN

p. 199: USDA Hardiness Zone Map—Davin Risk
p. 200: Seed packet labels—Davin Risk
Everything else: Gayla Trail

## SPECIAL THANKS

Thanks go out to Leela Corman for her lovely illustration work. And to Sarah Hood for her encouragement, use of her garden, and for hooking me up with other gardens and gardeners. To Allison Hladkyj and Sandy Gillians for use of their gardens. To Grahame Beakhust for the amazing and incredibly generous marathon tour of Ward's Island. Thanks to Colette of Urban Harvest. And to my awesome brother, Jason, whom I can always count on. Shout out to the Parkdale Community Beer Garden gang. Our garden rules! Thanks to Claire Robertson (loobylu.com) for the lush illustrations done in the mock-up stage.

I want to thank Beate Schwirtlich and all the **YouGrow Girl.com** gals and guys who have supported the project over the years or offered their time with copyedits, articles, photos, garden journals, etc. This book would not have happened without you or your enthusiasm.

I could not have pulled this book off alone. Super-extra-special thanks to Sarah Sockit and Davin Risk. You both worked so hard, and at a moment's notice, to meet impossible deadlines. This was no small feat. I am eternally grateful.

Designer, photographer, and gardener Gayla Trail is the creator of the acclaimed gardening website **www.YouGrowGirl.com**. Her work has been featured in magazines and newspapers and on radio across North America. Gayla lives in Toronto, where she and her partner, Davin Risk, run their design studio, Fluffco.

Gayla's love for gardening began with parsley seeds planted in a foam cup when she was five years old. Inspired by the potato plants her grandmother grew in a bucket on her senior center's fire escape, Gayla has always gardened in whatever space she had available. She now splits her gardening time between a rooftop deck, a community garden plot, and a formerly barren patch of public land on a busy urban corner.